Orwell and Gissing

American University Studies

Series IV
English Language and Literature

Vol. 185

PETER LANG
New York • Washington, D.C./Baltimore • Boston
Bern • Frankfurt am Main • Berlin • Vienna • Paris

Mark Connelly

Orwell and Gissing

PETER LANG
New York • Washington, D.C./Baltimore • Boston
Bern • Frankfurt am Main • Berlin • Vienna • Paris

Library of Congress Cataloging-in-Publication Data

Connelly, Mark.
Orwell and Gissing / Mark Connelly.
p. cm. — (American University studies. Series IV, English language and literature; 185)
Includes bibliographical references (p.   ) and index.
1. Orwell, George, 1903–1950. 2. Literature and society—England—History. 3. Authors, English—20th century—Biography. 4. Dickens, Charles, 1812–1870—Influence. 5. Gissing, George, 1857–1903—Influence. 6. Influence (Literary, artistic, etc.) 7. Utopias in literature. I. Title. II. Series: American university studies. Series IV, English language and literature; vol. 185.
PR6029.R8Z6264   828'.91209—dc21   97-8499
ISBN 0-8204-3330-6
ISSN 0741-0700

Die Deutsche Bibliothek-CIP-Einheitsaufnahme

Connelly, Mark:
Orwell and Gissing / Mark Connelly.
–New York; Washington, D.C./Baltimore; Boston; Bern;
Frankfurt am Main; Berlin; Vienna; Paris: Lang.
(American university studies: Ser. 4, English language and literature; Vol. 185)
ISBN 0-8204-3330-6 Gb.

Cover design by Nona Reuter.

© 1997 Peter Lang Publishing, Inc., New York

All rights reserved.
Reprint or reproduction, even partially, in all forms such as microfilm, xerography, microfiche, microcard, and offset strictly prohibited.

OTHER BOOKS BY MARK CONNELLY

The Diminished Self: Orwell and the Loss of Freedom

The Sundance Reader

CONTENTS

ONE	INTRODUCTION	1
TWO	BORN EXILES	9
THREE	DICKENS: THE HERITAGE	27
FOUR	ART AND CASH: *KEEP THE ASPIDISTRA FLYING* AND *NEW GRUB STREET*	39
FIVE	THE WOMAN BUSINESS	53
SIX	THE RAGGED REGIMENT: *A CLERGYMAN'S DAUGHTER* AND *THE ODD WOMEN*	69
SEVEN	DOOMED UTOPIAS: *ANIMAL FARM* AND *DEMOS*	83
EIGHT	LEAVES OF GRASS	97
NINE	CONCLUSION	115
	BIBLIOGRAPHY	119
	INDEX	123

ONE
INTRODUCTION

> Orwell had a thoroughly professional approach to writing and a finished style, though his literary judgements were sometimes eccentric...he would canvass Gissing, quite seriously, as the greatest English novelist.
>
> Anthony Powell

George Orwell left an enduring legacy. His sixty-year-old novels continually reappear in fresh editions. The pre-war essays about British imperialism "A Hanging" and "Shooting an Elephant" are still included in freshman anthologies as models of rhetorical clarity. The collapse of Communism in Russia and Eastern Europe created a new readership for *Animal Farm* and *Nineteen Eighty-Four* as intellectuals in emerging democracies struggled with their Stalinist heritage. In America debates about political correctness and campus speech codes frequently evoke the Orwellian terms "Big Brother" and "thought police."

Orwell is still read because he wrote about enduring issues—the independence of the self, the impact of technology, the loss of nature, poverty, sexuality, the decline of religious faith. Unlike most political writers in his ideologically-charged era, Orwell looked beyond immediate crises and the intense doctrinal debates of the Left to probe the larger *historical* forces at work in the twentieth century. Orwell sensed that science, technology, and mass communications were causing glacial shifts in human existence, radically altering the basic fabric of family life, the individual's relationship to society, humanity's relationship to the environment. These forces, he believed, would markedly change the nature of civilization, no matter which political system harnessed them.

In examining these deeper issues, Orwell was often ahead of his contemporaries. Commissioned by the Left Book Club in 1937 to document economic conditions in the depressed north of England, Orwell produced a book that dismayed his Socialist editors but outlined concerns expressed by environmentalists and social commentators a half-century later. In *The Road to Wigan Pier* Orwell graphically depicted the mean griminess of slum life but questioned the human cost of "progress." Observing that poor people were systematically deloused before being admitted into new government housing, Orwell noted, ". . . it is the kind of thing that makes you wish that the word 'hygiene' could be dropped out of the dictionary. Bugs are bad, but a state of affairs in which men will allow themselves to be dipped like sheep is worse" (71).

In that pre-nuclear, pre-environmentally conscious era the Left saw reform largely in terms of "science" and "progress." Socialists championed the production statistics flowing from Stalin's Five Year Plans as evidence of Communism's success. Visions of the future depicted glittering modern cities, massive hydroelectric plants, mass communications, electric appliances, and super highways. Unlike capitalism, Socialism would exploit natural resources for the benefit of humanity instead of a wealthy elite. Communing with nature, therefore, was often dismissed as a dangerous anachronism, a barrier to progress. Orwell, however, argued that technology should be accepted cautiously, like an addictive drug which is "useful, dangerous and habit-forming" (*Road* 169). The landscaped, glass and tile industrial parks that were beginning to appear in the 1930s did not comfort Orwell, despite their obvious improvement over the smoky factories of the nineteenth century. "It is important to remember this," he cautioned readers, "because there is always a temptation to think that industrialism is harmless so long as it is clean and orderly" (99). His sentiment that "In a healthy world there would be no demand for tinned food, aspirins, gramophones, gaspipe chairs, machine guns, daily newspapers, telephones, motorcars etc. etc. . . ." (170) sounds more New Age or New Left than the Old Left wedded to smokestack Socialism. Lenin had argued that Socialism plus electricity would equal Communism. But Orwell questioned the value of the "queer spectacle of modern electrical science" pointing out that, "Twenty million people are underfed but literally everyone in England has access to a radio"(84). For millions of people, he observed, the blaring of a radio has become "not only a more acceptable but a more *normal* background to their thoughts than the lowing of cattle or the song of birds" (170).

The slums Orwell described sixty years ago have disappeared, but his observations about technology and human liberty, pollution and progress, shoddy materialism and happiness remain relevant in the post-Socialist era.

One irony of Orwell's currency is that so many diverse people claim him as one of their own. Orwell is quoted by neo-Conservatives, champions of human rights, Catholics, environmentalists, old-line Socialists, and libertarians. Rigorously honest, Orwell recorded his ideas without self-censorship. Never attempting to be politically correct, Orwell was not afraid of voicing conflicting or eccentric views. "I should like to put it on record that I have never been able to dislike Hitler," Orwell stated flatly in his 1940 review of *Mein Kampf* (*CEJL* II 13). "I have reflected," he wrote, "that I would certainly kill him if I could get within reach of him, but that I could feel no personal animosity. The fact is that there is something deeply appealing about him" (II 13). In "Shooting an Elephant" Orwell confessed that while he detested the injustices of the British Raj, he also thought that "the greatest joy in the world would be to drive a bayonet into a Buddhist priest's guts" (*CEJL* I 236).

His honesty and his refusal to automatically follow a party line led Orwell to make contradictory statements. At times he adopted the standard Socialist line of his day, asserting that only a political and economic restructuring of society could improve the lot of humanity. At others he embraced Dickens' view that a moral "change of heart" was needed. Orwell wanted progress but distrusted science. He detested Nazism but opposed the Nuremberg trials and the "monstrous peace settlement . . . forced on Germany." Orwell saw nationalist sentiments as jingoist barriers to universal brotherhood but was irked by the Americanization of wartime Britain. He defended Dickens' moralist stance but ridiculed Gandhi's. Although an agnostic, he believed the central dilemma underlying the twentieth century was the loss of religious faith.

These contradictions have puzzled three generations of critics. Orwell's political detractors have long cited his inconsistencies as evidence of a neurotic misanthropy that invalidated his criticism of the Left. His supporters argue these fluctuations indicate that Orwell operated on a deeper philosophical plane. His contradictions, they state, stem from a conflict described as being moral, psychological, or existential in nature.

Jasbir Jain defined this conflict as Orwell's struggle to reconcile morality with technological progress, which aided humanity at the expense of human liberty (99). Gordon Beadle and Gregory Ashe, among others, suggested Orwell was basically a believer in the underdog version of Christian morality. His political sympathies shifted with the loss or acquisition of power so that after VE Day he saw little purpose in pursuing defeated Nazis. "Only the minority of sadists, who must have their 'atrocities' from one source or another, take a keen interest in the hunting-down of war criminals," he wrote in "Revenge is Sour" (*CEJL* IV 5). "Somehow the punishment of these monsters ceases to seem attractive when it becomes possible: indeed, once under lock and key, they almost cease to be monsters," he contended (IV 5). Richard Rees believed Orwell, like Simone Weil, consciously altered political loyalties to achieve a moral balance (6). Rees was one of the first critics to apply the term "existentialist" to Orwell. "He was in real life," Rees asserted, "a better existentialist, more authentic and more 'engaged,' than many philosophers whose existentialism exists mainly between the covers of a book" (8-9). More recently, Michael Carter described Orwell's life and career as an "existential progress" toward an "authentic identity."

Carter, like other scholars, prefaces his remarks on Orwell by citing George Woodcock's often quoted observation of Orwell's critics:

> When people of widely differing viewpoints—conservatives and Anarchists, Socialists and liberals, aging academics and young writers born old—find encouragement for their attitudes in a single author's work, we can reasonably assume that each of them is missing something, and that the work, considered as a whole, must be a good deal more complex than it appears at first sight. Orwell did not seek to be all things to all men; far from it. And if today he arouses echoes in such various minds, it is due more than anything else to the paradoxical fact in aspiring to make his prose pure and transparent, he wrote with an appearance of simplicity which concealed the protean complexity that often characterized his thoughts and arguments.
>
> A great deal of this complexity came from the fact that Orwell was a man who tended to glory in his contradictions and in the unsystematic nature of his thought. He was the last of a nineteenth-century tradition of individualist radicals which bred such men as Hazlitt, Cobbett and Dickens. He tended to move rather eccentrically and elusively between

> the poles of opinion to which most men remain tethered once they have taken up an attitude at the end of youth; in his most radical moods he was never afraid to sound what seemed to his critics the jarring note of conservatism. . . . His own limitations of thought and feeling, his obsessions and enthusiasms, were always personal and temperamental rather than partisan and theoretical. . . . he was never in any sense a party man, and the allegiances he acknowledged did not prevent him from expressing highly unorthodox opinions. (55-56)

Among Orwell's personal obsessions and enthusiasms was an abiding fascination with his favorite novelist, George Gissing. A late-Victorian novelist, Gissing was largely out of fashion and out of print in the 1930s and 1940s. His seemingly convention-bound novels about convention-bound Victorians struggling with nineteenth-century sexual morals and turn-of-the-century commercialism excited little interest among Depression-era critics and scholars. To Orwell's friends and colleagues, Gissing represented simply another one of Orwell's eccentric interests.

Learning of Orwell's death, Malcolm Muggeridge noted in his diary, "Thought much about his curious character, the complete unreality of so much of his attitude, his combination of intense romanticism with a dry interest in some of the dreariest aspects of life—e.g. Gissing" (qtd. Coppard & Crick 269). Anthony Powell remembered that Orwell's "imagination strayed back into the Victorian age" in both conversation and life (qtd. Coppard & Crick 241). Orwell, he recalled, delighted in his North London apartment because "it conjured up those middle-to-lower-middle-class nineteenth-century households on which his mind loved to dwell, particularly enthroned in the works of his favourite novelist, George Gissing" (241). Commenting on Orwell's life, Russell Kirk noted, "In a number of ways—his origins, his poverty, his pessimism, his mingled hatred and pity for the poor, in the subjects of his books—he resembles George Gissing, who died at a similar age of a similar cause after a similar life" (21).

Orwell's critics and biographers continually note the striking similarities between Orwell and his favorite writer. Both were lean, mustached consumptives who were products of the struggling middle class. Although both were destined by training and temperament for academic study, neither completed a university education. Both endured poverty and were estranged from the literary circles of their day. Orwell's contempt for the Auden-Isherwood camp in the 1930s paralleled Gissing's disdain for Oscar Wilde and the *fin de siècle* aesthetes. Both hated the slick superficiality of modern life with its mass-produced culture and mind-deadening advertising. As unhappy as they were with the state of society, they distrusted those bent on change. Both were "men of no party" who felt at odds with their times. Both wrote novels about quirky, often self-defeating outcasts who wage eccentric losing battles against conformity.

Since Orwell's death, Gissing has been rediscovered and resurrected. All of his twenty-four novels have been reprinted. Since 1970 over half a dozen substantial biographies have appeared, along with a Gissing newsletter. As in other things, Orwell, who also was an early admirer of Henry Miller, was ahead of his time, a pioneer Gissing scholar.

To fully understand Orwell, his character and conflicts, it is important to appreciate his relationship with his favorite novelist. Gissing served as both role model and alter-ego. Gissing provided Orwell with a touchstone to his beliefs, his pessimism, his British parochialism, his love of Dickens and cozy corners, his distaste for commercialism, his suspicion of "progress," his nagging penury, his restless sexuality.

TWO
BORN EXILES

> Both Gissing and Orwell . . . shared the melancholy distinction of men who see the world moving in a direction uncongenial to them.
>
> Richard Rees

In the last years of his life, George Orwell found solace in the novels of George Gissing. Orwell had dedicated his career to documenting the abuses of colonialism, the suffering of the unemployed, the misuse of capital, the rise of totalitarianism. He slept in public shelters with homeless men, shared meals of bread and tea with miners, and survived months of trench warfare during the Spanish Civil War. Severely wounded by a Fascist sniper, Orwell barely escaped Barcelona before being arrested by Communists. Disregarding diplomacy, popular Leftist sentiments, and wartime expediency, he attacked the Stalinist perversion of Socialism in *Animal Farm* while Britain was allied with the Soviet Union. His essays gained a reputation for clarity and honesty, which led V. S. Pritchett to call him the "wintry conscience of a generation." Disillusioned by postwar events and weakened by advancing tuberculosis, Orwell struggled to complete his last novel *Nineteen Eighty-Four*, a grim posthistorical account of humanity's loss of freedom, dignity, and individual identity.

"In the shadow of the atomic bomb it is not easy to talk confidently about progress," Orwell noted soberly. But, he observed, "there are many reasons, and George Gissing's novels are among them, for thinking that the present age is a good deal better than the last one" (*CEJL* IV 428-429). About Gissing, Orwell observed that "one can hardly read his descriptions of lower-middle-class life, so obviously truthful in their dreariness, without feeling that we have improved perceptibly on that black-coated, money-ruled world of only sixty years ago" (IV 429). As grim as London appeared in Orwell's novels, he seemed grateful that Gissing's "fog-bound, gas-lit London . . . where clothes, architecture and furniture had reached their rock-bottom of ugliness" was "almost as distant as that of Dickens" (429).

Orwell was fascinated with Gissing. "I am a great fan of his," he wrote Julian Symons in 1948, asserting, "I think *The Odd Women* is one of the best novels in English" (*CEJL* IV 416). Observing that no satisfactory biography of Gissing then existed, he called it "a job that is crying out to be done" (*CEJL* IV 438). He even considered writing one himself but was unable to undertake the necessary research. Orwell deeply regretted that he was never able to locate a copy of Gissing's novel *Born in Exile*. Over the years he had read library editions of Gissing's masterpiece *New Grub Street* but longed to possess a personal copy. Toward the end of his life, this book search became an obsession. Having exhausted British sources by 1949, he asked friends in New York to search America for a copy (*CEJL* IV 474). When Orwell wrote Richard Rees that April, he was seriously ill, having less than a year to live. He was tired, frustrated by his lingering illness and inability to work. But his spirits were lifted because "someone in the USA has managed to get me a copy of *New Grub Street* at last" (*CEJL* IV 498). In closing, Orwell admonished Rees not to lose his copy of *The Odd Women*. Two weeks later, Orwell wrote Anthony Powell of his find and expressed his hope that a publisher could be persuaded to reissue it (*CEJL* IV 499). "Everything of Gissing's—except perhaps one or two books written toward the end of his life—contains memorable passages," Orwell claimed in a 1948 article (*CEJL* IV 429).

Critics observed Orwell's affinity with his favorite author as early as 1936. Reviewing Orwell's second novel for the *New York Herald Tribune Books*, Vincent McHugh described Orwell's protagonist in *A Clergyman's Daughter* as a heroine of "a minor novel in Gissing's tradition" (qtd. Stansky & Abrahams 89). "The motto for this novel might have been taken from George Gissing's reflection on the 'life which is not lived for living's sake as all life should be, but under the goad of fear'" McHugh wrote (89). In Orwell's novel, McHugh saw familiar Gissing themes "the rigid round of custom, the loneliness, the causeless ennui" (90).

Since Orwell's death, scholars have come to share his admiration for Gissing, noting striking similarities between the two English writers. In his preface to the Penguin edition of *New Grub Street*, Bernard Bergonzi parenthetically noted the book's resemblance to Orwell's *Keep the Aspidistra Flying*, "which reads rather like a pastiche of *New Grub Street* transplanted to the London of the early nineteen thirties" (21). Robert L. Selig even noted the influence of Gissing on Orwell's futuristic novel:

> Even Orwell's best known work, *Nineteen Eighty-Four* (1949), seems full of Gissing touches, as Winston Smith trudges through an anti-utopian London of bad smells, bad plumbing, and degraded city "proles." From Gissing to Orwell, from 1891 to 1984, the distance is far less than one might have supposed. (138)

Orwell scholars have long commented on the similarity of the two writers. In his opening pages of *George Orwell: Fugitive From the Camp of Victory*, Richard Rees included a comparison to Gissing:

> His passion for literature was lifelong and dated from very early years; and if we consider only his first three deeply pessimistic novels he appears in some ways to resemble George Gissing. He has the same resolute, plodding honesty. . . (9)

J.R. Hammond stated that Orwell's novels "owe much to Gissing" (100). Like many critics, Hammond drew specific parallels between *Keep the Aspidistra Flying* and *New Grub Street* and *A Clergyman's Daughter* and *The Odd Women*. He also noted a remarkable likeness in Gissing's attitude toward nature and the English countryside in *The Private Papers of Henry Ryecroft* and that expressed by Orwell in *Coming Up for Air*.

The parallels between the life and work of George Orwell (1903-1950) and George Gissing (1857-1903) are striking. Both were products of the struggling middle class, enduring to some extent the same "poor boy at public school" stigma. Gissing was thirteen when his father died; he came of age in a widow's household with its pervading sense of loss and financial insecurity. Orwell did not lose his father, but his early retirement forced the family to maintain middle-class pretensions on a civil service pension. As young adults both men suffered extreme poverty and both experienced true hunger. They were deeply affected by the sights, sounds, and especially the smells of slum life which colored their novels. Both detested the capitalistic system they lived in, but they could not bring themselves to wholly commit themselves to an ideological alternative. As "men of no party" they stood apart from the literary cliques of their day. Neither completed a university education. Both felt exiled from and hostile to trendy literary circles. As novelists, both were greatly influenced by Dickens, whom they praised in critical studies. As much as they disliked the ugliness of the industrial age, they expressed a shared distaste for the sleekness and shininess of the new age. Both satirized the texture of middle-class values, advertising, popular literature, fashion, and cuisine. Hostile critics have used similar phrases in their denunciations, commonly accusing Orwell and Gissing of being wrongheaded, dreary, and misanthropic.

In concluding his biography of Gissing, John Halperin described Gissing as an exile in uniquely Orwellian terms:

> Gissing's bad luck, his masochism, his restlessness, his guilt, his insecurity, prevented him from feeling at home in *any* class—indeed made him feel, as Walter Allen has said, "permanently estranged, at odds with society," the ultimate outsider. . . . Always he felt the need to prove, or disprove, something: and so he worked himself to death.
> (362)

These similarities should not obscure the essential difference between Gissing and Orwell. Both men entered the world of the London slums in their twenties. The experience shaped their literary careers, their world view, their attitudes toward the poor, politics, and popular culture. But they entered poverty under radically different circumstances.

Orwell's "descent", if not calculated, resulted from a series of conscious actions. Although educated at Eton, he decided against attending university. Instead of pursuing higher education, he joined the Imperial Police and served in Burma for five years. He resigned from colonial service to become a writer, adopting his famous pseudonym in the process. Eager to explore poverty, Orwell costumed himself in tramp clothes to document the plight of the poor and homeless. At one point he feared his educated accent might prevent him from being accepted by the tramps he chose to befriend and chronicle. In 1931 he actually set out to get arrested for public drunkenness. His essay "Clink" records this amateur attempt at undercover investigative reporting.

Deliberately drunk, Orwell plodded the pavement in search of an arresting officer. Confronted by two policemen, he provided them with his assumed identity, Edward Burton, discharged clerk. But, as Orwell lamented, he got no further in his search than police court. ". . . I made several more attempts to get into trouble by begging under the noses of the police, but I seemed to bear a charmed life—no one took any notice of me" (*CEJL* I 94). Not wanting to get into serious trouble, Orwell broke off the experiment. "The trip, therefore, was more or less a failure," he concluded, "but I have recorded it as a fairly interesting experience" (94). One item of interest was the manner in which the police took him into custody, ". . . it amused me very much to see the cunning way in which they persuaded me along, never once disclosing the fact that they were making for the police station"(87).

Although half a century earlier, Gissing "seems to have enjoyed the prospect of prowling about the streets in workman's clothing in search of material" (Korg 45), he would have found nothing amusing about a police station. It was his arrest for theft that traumatically and irrevocably terminated his academic career and permanently changed the course of his life.

Unlike Orwell, Gissing was highly suited to school life. Born in Wakefield in 1857, Gissing became obsessed with academic achievement at an early age. Because his father died when he was thirteen, Gissing saw that his future success and security depended on achieving scholarships. Short of funds to support her five children, Gissing's mother was forced to sell her husband's shop and the family home. The town raised money to send the Gissing children to school. George Gissing proved to be a dedicated student; his self-imposed regimen was rigorous and unyielding. Limiting himself to five and a half hours sleep a night, he read through Shakespeare three times before he was sixteen (Halperin 14-15). According to Jacob Korg, Gissing turned down a theater invitation "because the thought of the study time he was missing would make him writhe in his seat throughout the performance" (11). Gissing excelled in his studies, winning numerous academic awards. One year he received so many books as prizes he had to hire a cab to carry them home (Gissing, *Collected Letters,* 1 32). He achieved the highest ranking in the Manchester district in the Oxford Local Examination in 1872, earning a three year scholarship to Owens College. In the 1870s Owens College served as a combination secondary school and college, preparing students for advanced studies at Oxford, Cambridge, or London University. Gissing studied eighteen hours a day, winning awards for English poetry, German, Latin, and Greek. Scoring high marks on University of London examinations, he achieved national awards in English, Latin, and history. These were matched with additional prizes from Owens College. Faculty and fellow students predicted he was destined for a brilliant career as a scholar and professor (Halperin 12-16).

During his last term at Owens, Gissing's disciplined life of study and academic accomplishment disintegrated. One day in 1876 he showed a friend named Morley Roberts the photograph of a young girl who, in Roberts' words, was "undoubtedly not a lady" (qtd. Halperin 17). Gissing had fallen in love with Marianne Helen Harrison. "Nell" Harrison was a seventeen-year-old prostitute Gissing had picked up in a tavern. Hopelessly infatuated, he was an easy mark for Nell and her landlady pimp. Soon he became Nell's lover as well as customer. Motivated by adolescent lust or naive idealism, he sought to rescue Nell. Roberts observed Gissing's growing obsession, noting that he "haunted the streets which she haunted, and sometimes saw her with other men" (qtd. Halperin 17). When Roberts suggested he break off the relationship, Gissing rebuked his friend for speaking ill of the future Mrs. Gissing.

Another friend, John George Black, wrote Gissing a shamefaced letter, confessing that while Gissing was absent he had slept with Nell. A few weeks later Black wrote again, anxiously detailing in clinical terms the symptoms of a venereal infection and asking Gissing for the name of a doctor. But Gissing's passion for Nell was unchecked by her profession or his own dose of gonorrhea. Whether driven by desire or sympathy, Gissing desperately attempted to keep Nell off the streets by supplying her with money. Hoping to reform her, Gissing took her on short trips and resolved to marry her. He invested in a sewing machine, offering Nell an alternative to prostitution. But she was an incurable alcoholic in constant need of drink money. Gissing pursued the relationship, neglecting his studies for the first time in his life. Out of funds, he sold his father's watch. Then in desperation, he began pilfering a student cloak room. Foolishly repeating the thefts, he began stealing coats as well as their contents. Learning of the thefts, the college hired a detective who caught the honor student in the act of stealing (Halperin 17-18). As biographer Halperin writes, on May 31, 1876 "Gissing's world came crashing down upon him" (18).

Gissing was arrested, tried, and convicted. His sexual liaison with a street prostitute was exposed. Expelled from Owens College and stripped of his awards, Gissing was sentenced to a month at hard labor. His academic career terminated and his job prospects shadowed by scandal, Gissing evoked some measure of sympathy. The college administration provided funds. Friends and family suggested he seek a new life in the New World.

Arriving in Boston in 1876, Gissing was impressed with America, inventions such as the telephone, the spirited Presidential election, central heating, and the well-stocked public libraries (Halperin 21). He envisioned pursuing a literary career. Needing money, he took a job teaching foreign languages at a high school in Waltham, Massachusetts. Although he apparently enjoyed teaching, Gissing abruptly left a few months later either because school officials learned of the Owens debacle or because he feared becoming involved with a female pupil (Halperin 21).

Gissing moved to Chicago where be began his writing career with a short story "Sins of the Fathers" published in a weekend supplement of *The Chicago Tribune*. In the following months Gissing published seventeen stories in newspapers. His success did not last long. Out of ideas for new stories and short of money, Gissing ended his American *Wanderjahr*, returned to England, his writing career, and Nell.

Gissing's relationship with Nell was stormy. Lack of money for alcohol drove her back to prostitution, and the couple was turned out of lodgings on numerous occasions. Undaunted, Gissing pursued writing, laboring to produce a 1,100 page novel entitled *Workers in the Dawn*.

At this time Gissing was attracted to Positivism and viewed himself as a "social novelist." Like Orwell's first book *Down and Out in Paris and London*, written a half century later, Gissing's first novel exposed his readers to the depths of poverty. "My special study," he wrote his brother, "is social science . . . everything I read I make subservient to this aim—the acquisition of a knowledge of the history of society" (*Letters* 1 224). *Workers in the Dawn* had a clear political message:

> The book, in the first place, is not a novel in the in the generally-accepted sense of the word, but a strong (possibly *too* plain-spoken) attack upon certain features of our present religious and social life which to *me* appear highly condemable. First & foremost, I attack the criminal negligence of governments which spend their time over matters of relatively no importance, to the neglect of the terrible social evils which should have been grappled with. Herein I am a mouthpiece of the advanced Radical party. (*Letters*, 1 281-282)

Gissing's radicalism was short-lived. Though disturbed by the poverty he was forced to confront, as Jacob Korg noted, Gissing was suspicious of political reform:

> . . . Gissing was a liberal of the school of Bentham, Owen, and Mill; yet he could not accept the egalitarian reform measures that followed

from their theories. On the contrary, he shared with Carlyle a profound distrust of democracy, and he echoed, in a somewhat altered and much vaguer form, Carlyle's faith in the elect. (41)

Unlike Orwell, who ended his first book with a list of political remedies for the worst social inequities, Gissing advocated a distinctly moral response based on classic sensibilities. Writing his brother Algernon regarding *Workers in the Dawn*, he outlined his personal remedy for the slums he described:

> Someone owns all these slums & alleys, & draws endless rent from them. Such owners would, in a better social state, be discovered & "Boycotted." Think what a force this same public opinion was in the best time of the Roman Republic, witnessed by the rigorous institution of the Censorship, which controlled almost every circumstance of a citizen's life & action. We need not have a personal Censor, but we can have the *Spirit* pervading our institutions, & to that it must come.
> (*Letters* 1 47)

Though deeply troubled by the plight of the poor, Gissing was not in favor of giving them a greater voice. "It is a fact, regrettable though it be, that scarcely one man in ten thousand is capable of original thought," he wrote Algernon in 1879 (*Letters* 1 45). Gissing's early disenchantment with reform attempts led him to abandon Positivism. According to Korg, when Gissing's mentor Frederic Harrison "prodded him for some statement of principles and some positive views about social reform, Gissing had none to offer, for his views and his principles were already being undermined by the tormenting actuality reflected in his novel" (42).

The protagonist of *Workers in the Dawn* is Arthur Golding, a sensitive artist torn between dedication to radical politics and his instinctive love of painting. He also struggles with Carrie, a young girl of the streets he marries and attempts to reform. But Carrie, like Nell, is a hopeless alcoholic. She continues to drink, refusing to abandon her prostitute friends who urge her to kill

Golding for his inheritance. Gissing depicted Golding's attempt at reforming his wife as a naive endeavor that becomes a soul-crushing burden.

Gissing completed his novel, *then* married Nell Harrison, apparently resigning himself to the fate of his hero. Like the fictional Carrie, Nell "not only was. . . ignorant, foolish, wilful, and defiant, but . . . was also both vulgar and slovenly" (Halperin 31). The marriage was a disaster. Within two years the couple separated. Gissing had his wife hospitalized, but she escaped and dunned him mercilessly for support. She died at thirty of drink and exposure, having pawned her wedding ring.

Loneliness and sexual frustration drove Gissing to a second disastrous union. His second wife, Edith Underwood, was a working class woman with little artistic sensibility. She bore Gissing two sons but made his life miserable with bouts of ill-temper that increasingly erupted into physical violence. Laboring to write, Gissing had to endure domestic turmoil, including rows with servants and a gas explosion. His wife became increasingly abusive and argumentative, leading Gissing to despair of ever feeling at home as evidenced in an 1893 diary entry:

> On way home, at night, an anguish of suffering in the thought that I can never hope to have an intellectual companion at home. Condemned for ever to associate with inferiors—and so crassly unintelligent. Never a word exchanged on anything but the paltry everyday life of the household. Never a word to me, for anyone, of understanding sympathy—or of encouragement. Few men, I am sure, have led so bitter a life. (*Journal* 295)

His wife's violent outbursts led to physical abuse, driving Gissing from his home. His separation from his second wife was tempestuous. Edith publicly threatened to kill a woman and struck a police officer. She was arrested in 1902 and declared insane. Sent to an asylum, she remained a mental patient until her death in 1917 (Halperin 360).

Throughout these years, Gissing supported himself by writing novels, nearly one a year, which were, in Orwell's words, "sweated out of him during his struggle towards a leisure which he never enjoyed. . ." (CEJL IV 436).

Though he found some comfort with a literary Frenchwoman, years of stress and possible syphilis took their toll. Exhausted and suffering from emphysema, Gissing died in France at the age of forty-six.

Commenting on Gissing's short, unhappy life, Orwell, who also would die at forty-six, mused ". . . we must be thankful for the piece of youthful folly which turned him aside from a comfortable middle-class career and forced him to become the chronicler of vulgarity, squalor and failure" (*CEJL* IV 436).

In the role of chronicler, Gissing produced novels that presaged much of Orwell's fiction a half century later. In commenting on Gissing, John Halperin described his work in terms that could just as accurately be applied to Orwell:

> Certainly some of his books do seem pertinent to the world of today. He hated advertising, the London tubes appalled him, and he could see where the manufacture of armaments would lead. He anticipated the role science was destined to play in our lives, detested the urban sprawl and the disfigurement of the countryside by industry, and was an ecologist before anyone knew what ecology was. But his responses were always intensely personal. (3)

The books Gissing produced appealed to Orwell because spiritually both novelists felt exiled, perhaps even persecuted by their environments. Writing to his brother Algernon in 1885, Gissing advised a kind of self-imposed exile:

> Keep apart, keep apart, & preserve one's soul alive, —that is the teaching for the day. It is ill to have been born in these times, but one can make world within a world. A glimpse of the morning or evening sky will give the right note, & then we must make what music we can.
> (*Letters* 2 349)

As Halperin observed, Gissing was at odds with his times:

> It is this aspect of Gissing's vision, the nervous reaction to the noise, dirt, and triviality of contemporary life, that I have called peculiarly "modern" —fuelled, of course, by hatred of the present, a temperamental preference for everything that is dead, dying, and gone. As he wished always to be somewhere other than where he was, so he recoiled from his own time with passion consistent and unflinching.
> (207)

Orwell shared Gissing's sense that he was living in the wrong time, that he was painfully out of step with his era. Woodcock noted that Orwell expressed the Anarchists' disenchantment with the twentieth century:

> . . . Orwell tended to see the present as a time of particular moral degeneracy. He looked forward with somewhat less confidence than they did to a better world in the future, but he shared their feeling that in past times, golden or at least silver ages, human existence had been more meaningful and more natural. (175)

Writing to his brother in 1880, Gissing commented bitterly on the times he felt condemned to endure:

> Our age, in fact, is thoroughly empty, mean, and windbaggish, & the mass of people care so little to find employment in intellectual matters that they are driven to all manner of wild physical excesses for the sake of excitement. (*Letters* I 312)

Sixty years later, Orwell despaired of his age, noting the mean-spirited ugliness of current intellectual discourse:

> We are all drowning in filth. . . . I feel that intellectual honesty and balanced judgement have simply disappeared from the face of the earth. . . . Everyone is dishonest, and everyone is utterly heartless toward people who are outside the immediate range of his own interests and sympathies. . . . All power is in the hands of paranoiacs. (*CEJL* II 423)

Biographers and critics view this common temperament played out in Gissing's and Orwell's fiction, particularly in the plight of their protagonists. Gissing's heroes are intellectual aristocrats, sensitive, perhaps hypersensitive young males with artistic interests who are invariably brought to grief. His heroes are often moody, misanthropic, suspicious, and hopelessly self-defeating:

> It is the focus on the individual confronted by circumstances, social and financial, beyond his control that gives such power to Gissing's best novels—the confrontation of men and economic systems, the brute force of money, the negation of the individual in a money-grubbing system. . . . Gissing's idealistic characters who are also impractical always come to bad ends. (Halperin 5-6)

Similarly, Woodcock views Orwell's characters as hopelessly doomed figures unable to rise above their oppressive environs:

> . . . the central figure of every Orwell novel is a solitary, detached by some scar in his past from the world in which he finds himself, compelled to live the double existence of the misfit, and, after inevitable and ineffectual rebellion, doomed to fail and be destroyed or finally and hopelessly to be enslaved. (58)

The striking note of comity between Gissing and Orwell's protagonists is their neurotic self-consciousness of their social and economic status. Gordon Comstock, Orwell's moth-eaten poet in *Keep the Aspidistra Flying*, has a paroxysm of angst over spending a three penny piece:

> Because how can you buy anything with a threepennybit? It isn't a coin, it's the answer to a riddle. You look such a fool when you take it out of your pocket, unless it's in among a whole handful of other coins. . . The shopgirl sniffs. She spots immediately that it's your last three-pence in the world. . . . And you stalk out with you nose in the air and can't ever go to that shop again. (4)

The hero of Gissing's *Born in Exile*, Godwin Peak, is equally distressed when he scrutinizes the "shamefaced change" in his pocket (59). Though a prize-winning student at Whitelaw College, Peak contemplates withdrawing when a vulgar uncle announces his intention to open "Peak's Dining and Refreshment Room" near the campus:

> If indeed that awful thing came to pass, farewell to Whitelaw! What possibility of pursuing his studies when every class-companion, every Professor,—nay, the very porters,—had become aware that he was nephew to the man who supplied the meals over the way? Moral philosophy had no prophylact against on ordeal such as this. (56)

Gissing's most pathetic case of shame-faced sensitivity occurs in *A Life's Morning.* James Hood, the father of the novel's heroine, finds a ten pound note in an old ledger belonging to his employer. Heading into town with plans to report his discovery, he is jostled by a drunk who knocks his hat out a train window. Unable to bear the stigma of walking about hatless—something Gissing again describes as an "ordeal"—Hood spends the bank note in order to buy a new hat. Now unable to return the original bill and fearful his story might not be credible, Hood decides to keep the change. Learning of the theft, Hood's lecherous employer makes sexual advances toward the heroine, threatening to discharge her father unless she submits. To protect his daughter's reputation, Hood commits suicide.

Sympathetic to his favorite novelist, Orwell went to lengths to defend this "particular tragedy" as being "entirely plausible in its context" because of Victorian dress codes. "Today," Orwell reasoned, "if you had somehow contrived to lose your trousers, you would probably embezzle money rather than walk about in your underpants (*CEJL* IV 431).

Orwell was keenly attuned to Gissing's outlook, his plight. If contemporaries dismissed Gissing as a gloomy misanthrope, Orwell understood and shared Gissing's frustrations:

> Behind his rage and querulousness there lay a perception that the horrors of life in late-Victorian England were largely unnecessary. The grime, the stupidity, the ugliness, the sex-starvation, the furtive debauchery, the vulgarity, the bad manners, the censoriousness—these things were unnecessary, since the puritanism of which they were a relic no longer upheld the structure of society. (*CEJL* IV 430)

Orwell also noted that Gissing "did not admire the working class as such, and he did not believe in democracy. He wanted to speak not for the multitude, but for the exceptional man, the sensitive man, isolated among barbarians" (*CEJL* IV 430). Orwell sensed that despite his experiences, Gissing lacked a political consciousness. Yet Orwell saw that Gissing's limited ideological development was compensated by a redeeming "honesty" of vision which made his reactionary stance and prejudices forgivable:

> In a mild way his outlook is reactionary, from lack of foresight rather than from ill-will. Having been obliged to live among them, he regarded the working class as savages, and in saying so he was merely being intellectually honest; he did not see that they were capable of becoming civilised if given slightly better opportunities. But, after all, what one demands from a novelist is not prophecy, and part of the charm of Gissing is that he belongs so unmistakably to his own time, although his time treated him badly. (*CEJL* IV 434)

Despite a limited political vision, Gissing, in Orwell's opinion, was a champion of the English novel ". . . .merely on the strength of *New Grub Street*, *Demos*, and *The Odd Women* I am ready to maintain that England has produced very few better novelists," he asserted (*CEJL* IV 433).

It is noteworthy that Orwell mentions these novels by name because they clearly influenced his own work. Two of his novels, as Hammond mentions, were largely based on *New Grub Street* and *The Odd Women*. *Demos*, subtitled *A Story of English Socialism*, Gissing's novel of a failed utopia provides a precursor to *Animal Farm*.

In theme, characterization, plot, and attention to gritty detail, Gissing's novels served as models to Orwell who shared his favorite novelist's sense of exile and belief that no simple solutions were likely to make society more hospitable to his lonely protagonists. As in Orwell's own novels, Gissing's heroes suffer because of civilization, not a specific political system or group of identifiable enemies. Orwell viewed this as a strength:

> It is a point in his favour that he had no very strong moral purpose. He had, of course, a deep loathing of the ugliness, emptiness, and cruelty of the society he lived in, but he was concerned to describe it rather than change it. There is usually no one in his books who can be pointed to as the villain, and even when there is a villain he is not punished.
> (*CEJL* IV 435)

In documenting the ugliness, emptiness, and cruelty of their societies, both Gissing and Orwell were greatly influenced by Dickens, whom both admired and wrote about. The affinity of Orwell and Gissing in critical literary temperament is demonstrated in Orwell's essay on Dickens in which he calls Gissing "the best of the writers on Dickens."

THREE
DICKENS: THE HERITAGE

> Dickens is one of those writers who are well-worth stealing.
>
> George Orwell

In a sense both Gissing and Orwell "stole" from Charles Dickens. As novelists, they admired Dickens' ability to capture scenes and create memorable characters. For Orwell, Dickens had attained the status of a national monument:

> ... he is an institution that there is no getting away from. How often one really thinks about any writer, even a writer one cares for, is a difficult thing to decide; but I should doubt whether anyone who has actually read Dickens can go a week without remembering him in one context or another. Whether you approve of him or not, he is *there*, like the Nelson Column. At any moment some scene or character, which may come from some book you cannot even remember the name of, is liable to drop into your mind. Micawber's letters! Winkle in the witness box! Mrs Gamp! Mrs Wititterly and Sir Tumley Snuffim! Todgers's! (George Gissing said that when he passed the Monument it was never of the Fire of London that he thought, always of Todger's.)
>
> (*CEJL* I 449)

Dickens' influence is keenly evident in Gissing's and Orwell's novels, particularly in their descriptions of poverty, especially the poverty of the London slums and their eccentric inhabitants.

Ironically, though both Gissing and Orwell were men at "odds with their times," they shared the perception that as bad as the social abuses were in their respective eras, they lived in an age much improved over Dickens'. Writing at the turn of the century, George Gissing believed that he lived in an time thankfully apart from that of Dickens':

> It was a time by several degrees harsher, coarser, and uglier than our own. . . . It was an age in which the English character seemed bent on exhibiting all its grossest and meanest and most stupid characteristics. Sheer ugliness of everyday life reached a limit not easily surpassed; thickheaded national prejudice, in consequence of great wars and British victories, had marvellously developed; aristocracy was losing its better influence, and power passing to a well-fed multitude, remarkable for a dogged practicality which, as often as not meant ferocious egoism.
> (Gissing *Dickens* 8-9)

In Gissing's view, Dickens chronicled a "time of ugliness: ugly religion, ugly law, ugly relations between rich and poor, ugly clothes, ugly furniture" (14). As disillusioned as Gissing was with the shabby commercialism and hypocritical conventions of late nineteenth-century society, he felt his era improved over Dickens'.

Forty years later, Orwell looked back on Gissing's era and labeled it the "rock-bottom of ugliness" characterized by stupidity, ugliness, vulgarity, and bad manners. Orwell stated that his era had "improved perceptibly" over the "black-coated, money-ruled world of only sixty years ago" (*CEJL* IV 429). Gissing's "fog-bound, gas-lit London" seemed to Orwell "almost as distant as that of Dickens" (*CEJL* IV 429).

Despite their claims of "perceptible" progress, Gissing's and Orwell's novels offer little evidence of improvement. Oliver

Twist would be quite at home in the slums Gissing depicted in his 1889 novel *The Nether World*. And he would be quite familiar with the London Orwell described in his Depression-era novels. Even in futuristic Oceania, Oliver Twist would recognize the landscape of London in *Nineteen Eighty-Four*, with its "vistas of rotting nineteenth-century houses, their sides shored up with balks of timber" and "sordid colonies of wooden dwellings like chicken houses"(7).

The influence Dickens had on Gissing and Orwell in creating atmosphere, developing descriptive texture, and fashioning narrative scope is readily apparent. Their London scenes, in particular, derive much from Dickens. Consider Oliver Twist's first glimpse of London as the Artful Dodger leads him to Fagin's den:

> A dirtier or more wretched place he had never seen. The street was very narrow and muddy, and the air was impregnated with filthy odours. There were a good many small shops; but the only stock in trade appeared to be heaps of children, who, even at that time of night, were crawling in and out at the doors, or screaming from the inside. The sole places that seemed to prosper amid the general blight of place were the public-houses, and in them the lowest orders of Irish were wrangling with might and main. Covered ways and yards, which here and there diverged from the main street, disclosed little knots of houses, where drunken men and women were positively wallowing in filth. . .
>
> (Dickens *Oliver Twist* 59)

Gissing's first novel, *Workers in the Dawn*, opens with a nearly identical scene as the narrator "walks" his reader through Whitecross Street:

> The fronts of the houses, as we glance up towards the deep blackness overhead, have a decayed, filthy, often an evil, look; and here and there, on either side, is a low, yawning archway, or a passage some four feet wide, leading presumably to human habitations. . . . Straining the eyes into horrible darkness, we behold a blind alley, the unspeakable abominations of which are dimly suggested by a gas-lamp

> flickering at the further end. . . . the good people of Whitecross Street are thirsty as well as hungry, and there is no lack of gin-palaces to supply their needs. Open the door and look into one of these. Here a group are wrangling over a disputed toss or bet, here two are coming to blows, there are half-a-dozen young men and women, all half-drunk, mauling each other with vile caresses. . . (3-6)

Orwell's characters encounter a London noticeably similar to Oliver Twist's. On her arrival in London, Dorothy Hare, the virginal heroine of *A Clergyman's Daughter*, wanders through "labyrinthine streets where snotty-nosed children played at hop-scotch on pavements horrible with banana skins and decaying cabbage leaves"(157). In *Keep the Aspidistra Flying* Gordon Comstock comes to live in a rooming house in a neighborhood where the "narrow pavements were smeared with a quantity of dogs' excrement"(209). The London Orwell envisioned for the world of 1984 differed little from the London Dickens had depicted a century and half before. In *Nineteen Eighty-Four* Winston Smith passes through "vague, brown-colored slums" reminiscent of those traversed by Oliver Twist:

> He was walking up a cobbled street of little two-story houses with battered doorways which gave straight on the pavement and which were somehow curiously suggestive of rat holes. There were puddles of filthy water here and there among the cobbles. In and out of the dark doorways, and down narrow alleyways that branched off on either side, people swarmed in astonishing numbers—girls in full bloom, with crudely lipsticked mouths, and youths who chased the girls, and swollen waddling women who showed you what the girls would be like in ten years time, and old bent creatures shuffling along on splayed feet, and ragged barefooted children who played in the puddles and then scattered at angry yells from their mothers. Perhaps a quarter of the windows in the street were broken and boarded up. Most of the people paid no attention to Winston; a few eyed him with a sort of guarded curiosity. . . .
> . . . . It was nearly twenty hours, and the drinking shops which the proles frequented ("pubs," they called them) were choked with customers. From their grimy swing doors, endlessly opening and

shutting, there came forth a smell of urine, sawdust, and sour beer. In an angle formed by a projecting house front three men were standing very close together, the middle one of them holding a folded-up newspaper which the other two were studying over his shoulders. . . . It was obviously some serious piece of news that they were reading. He was a few paces away from them when suddenly the group broke up and two of the men were in violent altercation. (70-72)

These passages exhibit a common pattern of development, attention to detail, and tone. Following a graphic description of extreme squalor, the inhabitants are revealed to be brutish "wrangling" subhumans prone to drink and violence. The authors' reactions express both fear and disgust. In all three scenes, the viewpoint is that of a shocked outsider. In all three passages, the poor are represented as a separate species who are granted no individual identity or compassion. Each author seems especially repulsed by the sexuality of the poor men and women "wallowing in filth" and "mauling each other with vile caresses."

Gissing's and Orwell's shared fascination with Dickens led them to devote their most ambitious works of literary criticism to him. In 1939 George Orwell wrote his longest critical essay on Charles Dickens at a time when many critics were eager to embrace this "institution" of an author and credit him as one of their own. "The Marxist," Orwell observed, "claims him as 'almost' a Marxist, the Catholic claims him as 'almost' a Catholic, and both claim him as a champion of the proletariat..." (*CEJL* I 414). Dickens, Orwell noted, was both widely appreciated and largely misunderstood. Examining Dickens in contrast to "the smelly little orthodoxies which are now contending for our souls," Orwell sought to define where Dickens stood "socially, morally, and politically" (*CEJL* I 415). In writing his essay, Orwell drew heavily on Gissing's 1897 book *Charles Dickens: A Critical Study*, stating that Gissing was "the best of the writers on Dickens" (*CEJL* I 414).

Orwell's essay builds on Gissing's observations of Dickens' political consciousness, his attitudes toward the poor, his social criticism, and remedies for reform. Above all, Orwell concurred with Gissing's view of what Dickens was *not*. He was not, as many casual readers and Leftist critics assumed, a champion of the proletariat. Orwell agreed with Gissing's observation that Dickens never depicted the "workman at war with capital," never including among his hundreds of characters a single "representative wage-earner...battling for bread and right" (Gissing, *Dickens* 242). Orwell, like Gissing, points out that Dickens' lone working class character, Stephen Blackpool in *Hard Times*, is very unconvincing, representing in Gissing's words "nothing at all."

Orwell explains that this absence was due in part to a factor of geography, supporting Gissing's observation that Dickens "did not know the north of England" (242). He was "a south of England man, and a cockney at that, and therefore out of touch with the bulk of the real oppressed masses, the industrial and agricultural labourers" (Orwell *CEJL* I 434). Orwell's comment that Dickens "sees the world as a middle-class world, and that everything outside these limits is either laughable or slightly wicked" (*CEJL* I 428) echoes Gissing's observation,"He was a member of the middle class, and as far from preaching 'equality' in its social sense as any man that ever wrote" (*Dickens* 259).

Orwell sensed that Dickens feared "the mob." The most memorable scenes in *A Tale of Two Cities* reveal Dickens' obsession with riot and mayhem, "The revolutionaries appear to him simply as degraded savages—in fact, as lunatics. He broods over their frenzies with a curious imaginative intensity" (*CEJL* I 422). In these comments Orwell builds on Gissing's view that "Dickens, for all his sympathy, could not look with entire approval on the poor grown articulate with their wrongs" (*Dickens* 258). "He was," Gissing wrote, "never a democrat; in his heart he always held that *to be governed* was the people's good; only let the governors be rightly chosen" (*Dickens* 238).

In addition, Orwell focused on Gissing's belief that Dickens was equally out of touch with science and technology, which were part of the industrial revolution and often hailed as oppressed humanity's salvation:

> What is more striking, in a seemingly "progressive" radical, is that he is not mechanically minded. He shows no interest either in the details of machinery or in the things machinery can do. As Gissing remarks, Dickens nowhere describes a railway journey with anything like the enthusiasm he shows in describing journeys by stage coach.
> (*CEJL* I 444).

Dickens, Orwell observed, "scarcely notes" inventions such as the telegraph, coal-gas, and India-rubber, which appeared in his lifetime. Dickens, Gissing and Orwell stated, did not intend to chronicle current events or economic conditions. He looked backwards. "His youth," Gissing noted, "belonged to the pre-locomotive time" (*Dickens* 38). Orwell concurred, stating, "In nearly all of his books one has a curious feeling that one is living in the first quarter of the nineteenth century, and in fact, he does tend to return to this period" (*CEJL* I 444).

Orwell shared Gissing's sense that Dickens was out of touch with the proletariat. He also agreed with Gissing's view that Dickens lacked a true grasp of history. In reviewing Dickens' *Childhood History of England*, Gissing states that Dickens "never attained to a theory of reform," that he detected no evolutionary pattern to historical events:

> Dickens had no serious historical knowledge, and no true understanding of what is meant by history; his volume shows a series of more or less grotesque sovereigns, who play pranks before high heaven at the expense of the multitudes they are supposed to rule by divine right . . . The past, to his mind, was much better forgotten. That the world progressed, he never for a moment held in doubt; but the rate of

progress was not at all in keeping with his energetic habits.

(*Dickens* 236-237)

Orwell came to much the same conclusion in examining Dickens' treatment of the French Revolution. Dickens, he saw, had no sense of what a Marxist might deem historical inevitability. Instead, he merely saw a series of actions brought about by the misdeeds of irresponsible monarchs. Like Gissing, Orwell focused on the fact that Dickens saw the entire revolution as an avoidable catastrophe:

> Dickens sees clearly enough that the French Revolution was bound to happen and that many of the people who were executed deserved what they got. If, he says, you behave as the French aristocracy had behaved, vengeance will follow . . .
>
> In other words, the French aristocracy had dug their own graves. But there is no perception here of what is now called historic necessity. Dickens sees that the results are inevitable, given the causes, but he thinks that the causes might have been avoided. . . . If the wicked nobleman could somehow have turned over a new life, like Scrooge, there would have been no Revolution, no *jacquerie*, no guillotine—and so much the better.
>
> (*CEJL* I 421-422)

For Orwell, Dickens' belief in "behavior" is the key to his message. In all his attacks on social institutions, be it welfare, justice, or education, "his target is not much society as 'human nature'" (*CEJL* I 416). Orwell stated that, "It would be difficult to point anywhere in his books to a passage suggesting that the economic system is wrong *as a system*"(*CEJL* I 416). The moral of *Hard Times* is that "capitalists ought to be kind, not that workers ought to be rebellious." In fact, Orwell saw that Dickens' "whole 'message' is one that at first glance looks like an enormous platitude: If men would behave decently the world would be decent" (*CEJL* I 417).

This leads Orwell to characterize the Dickens's hero as the "Good Rich Man":

This character belongs especially to Dickens's early optimistic period. He is usually a "merchant" . . . and he is always a superhumanly kindhearted old gentleman who "trots" to and fro, raising his employees' wages, patting children on the head, getting debtors out of jail and, in general, acting the fairy godmother (*CEJL* I 417).

Orwell's concept of the Good Rich Man is clearly derived from Gissing's perception that Dickens' remedy for social ills was not legislation or government action, but private acts of benevolence by good rich men:

His savior of society was a man of heavy purse and large heart, who did the utmost possible good in his own particular sphere . . . . With what gusto does he write of any red-cheeked old gentleman who goes about scattering half-sovereigns, and finding poor people employment, and brightening squalid sick-chambers with the finest produce of Covent Garden . . . . They are chubby fairies in tights and gaiters . . . . To double a clerk's salary is a mere bit of forenoon fun; after dinner, we picture them supplying fraudulent debtors with capital for a new undertaking, or purchasing an estate in Hampshire to be made over forthwith to the widow of some warehouse porter with sixteen children.
(*Dickens* 251-253)

The charitable merchant who gives away money as fast as he makes it is clearly a dream figure whom Gissing and Orwell found difficult to imagine that Dickens could really hold as credible. Both Gissing and Orwell focus on the Good Rich Man to symbolize Dickens' true reaction to the social ills his books documented.

Orwell described Dickens' response to oppression and injustice as a moral one, based on urging a "change of heart" rather than political reform. This follows Gissing's view of Dickens' heroes that, "Always it is the heart rather than the head" (*Dickens* 254). Orwell deems Dickens' radicalism to be of "the vaguest kind" because Dickens "has no constructive suggestions, not even a clear grasp of the nature of the society he is attacking, only an emotional perception that something is wrong. All he can finally say is, 'Behave decently'" (*CEJL* I 457-8). Here again Orwell developed his analysis of Dickens on Gissing's assessment:

> Dickens's remedy for the evils left behind by the bad old times was, for the most part, private benevolence. He distrusted legislation; he had little faith in charitable associations; though such work as that of the Ragged Schools strongly interested him . . . .
> . . . Stephen Blackpool in *Hard Times* would hold rebellion a sin; and as for the rank and file of hungry creatures, they seem never to have heard that there is movement in the land, that voices are raised on their behalf, and even to some purpose. No; their hope is in the Cheeryble brothers; not at all in Chartist or in Radical or in Christian Socialist. Very significant the omission. Dickens, for all his sympathy, could not look with entire approval on the poor grown articulate about their wrongs. He would not have used the phrase, but he thought the thought, that humble folk must know "their station."
> (*Dickens* 251-259)

As Orwell commented in his essay, Dickens is a moralist, not a radical. Despite all his ferocious attacks on the abusive hypocrisy of his times, he was ultimately pro-capitalist because his moral is "that capitalists ought to be kind, not that workers ought to be rebellious" (*CEJL* I 417).

Despite these "limitations" both Gissing and Orwell shared the view that Dickens largely succeeded because of his middle-class mentality. In Gissing's view, Dickens was "essentially a member of the great middle class, and on that very account able to do such work, to strike such blows, for the cause of humanity in his day and generation" (*Dickens* 259). Part of Dickens' success lay in his ability to relate to his readers:

> What is called the "popular conscience" was on Dickens's side; and he had the immense advantage of being able to raise a hearty laugh even whilst pointing to his lesson. Among the rarest of things is this thorough understanding between author and public, permitting a man of genius to say aloud with impunity that which all his hearers say within themselves dumbly, inarticulately . . . . Broadly speaking, he was one

of his readers, and therein lay his strength for reform.

(*Dickens* 130-133)

Orwell concurred with Gissing's definition of Dickens' unique relationship with his middle-class readership which made him both a critic of society and one of its cherished monuments:

> ... the very people he attacked have swallowed him so completely that he has become a national institution himself. In its attitude toward Dickens the English public has always been a little like the elephant which feels a blow with a walking-stick as a delightful tickling.
>
> (*CEJL* I 415)

Ultimately, both Gissing and Orwell shared the view that despite his inability to develop a systemic concept of social ills, his sentimentality, his absurd characters, Dickens is admirable because of his honesty and his refusal to embrace the shallow jingoism and prejudices of his times. "No grown-up person," Orwell wrote, "can read Dickens without feeling limitations, and yet there does remain his native generosity of mind, which acts as a kind of anchor and nearly always keeps him where he belongs" (*CEJL* I 459). "Whatever his mistakes and his defects," Gissing observed, "insincerity had no place among them" (*Dickens* 293).

Gissing concluded his volume on Dickens by quoting remarks made by Carlyle on learning of the author's death, "'The good, the gentle, high-gifted, ever-friendly, noble Dickens—every inch of him an honest man'" (*Dickens* 293). Orwell ended his critical essay with much the same tone, viewing Dickens as an admirable figure of great value, even in 1939. To capture the essence of Dickens, Orwell described what he called Dickens' "face behind the page":

> It is the face of a man who is always fighting against something, but who fights in the open and is not frightened, the face of a man who is *generously angry*—in other words, of a nineteenth-century liberal, a

free intelligence, a type hated with equal hatred by all the smelly little orthodoxies which are now contending for our souls. (460)

Writing at the end of the 1930s, Orwell built upon Gissing's observations seeking to defend Dickens' concept of personal morality, much maligned by the Left which advocated that good-hearted acts of charity were superficial placations. Facing the abuse of Socialism under Stalin and his loyal apologists, Orwell could not dismiss the validity of Dickens' moralism, which he viewed as half of a dialectic argument:

> . . . two viewpoints are always tenable. The one, how can you improve human nature until you have changed the system? The other, what is the use of changing the system before you have improved human nature?. . . . The moralist and the revolutionary are constantly undermining one another. . . . The central problem—how to prevent power from being abused—remains unsolved. Dickens, who had not the vision to see that private property is an obstructive nuisance, had the vision to see that. "If men would behave decently the world would be decent" is not such a platitude as it sounds.
>
> (*CEJL* I 428)

Orwell's essay, like Gissing's book, is the work of an admirer. Intellectually, Orwell and Gissing recognized Dickens' faults and limitations. As writers, however, they were impressed by his power to capture his era and impact readers. As men who were at odds with their times, their society, their counterparts, they sought attention, recognition, reader response. Dickens provided them both with a powerful role model. They sought to defend Dickens against the critics, who by 1903 and certainly by 1939, were likely to dismiss him as a mid-Victorian sentimentalist. For Gissing and Orwell, who both wrote novels about writers, Dickens was ultimately "a writer's writer."

FOUR
ART AND CASH: *KEEP THE ASPIDISTRA FLYING* AND *NEW GRUB STREET*

> To have money is becoming of more and more importance in a literary career; principally because to have money is to have friends.
> Gissing, *New Grub Street*

> Money, money, all is money. Could you write even a penny novelette without money to put heart in you? Invention, energy, wit, style, charm—they've all got to be paid for in hard cash... You can't even be friendly, you can't be civil, when you have no money in your pocket.
> Orwell, *Keep the Aspidistra Flying*

For George Orwell, *New Grub Street*, the novel he lovingly read and reread in soup-stained library editions, was Gissing's "most impressive" work which he regarded as an "upsetting and demoralizing book" (*CEJL* IV 431). As a novelist and journalist, Orwell naturally related to Gissing's nightmare of creative sterility—writer's block. "No doubt," Orwell noted, "the number of writers who suddenly lose the power to write is not large, but it is a calamity that *might* happen to anybody at any moment, like sexual impotence" (*CEJL* IV 431).

New Grub Street was the obvious influence of Orwell's novel *Keep the Aspidistra Flying* which replays Gissing's drama of an outcast writer who wages a futile battle against society, refuses assistance from friends, and wallows masochistically in poverty, grimly determined to grind out hackwork even he detests. The impact of *New Grub Street* is unmistakable. As Jeffrey Meyers observed, "Orwell's acknowledged master and (sometimes baneful) model for the novel of poverty is George Gissing. . ."(88).

The Gissing influence helps to explain the confusions and flaws in Orwell's third novel. Writing a "novel of poverty" in the depths of the Depression, Orwell chose an highly unrepresentative protagonist. Gordon Comstock is a poet—not a laid off factory worker or struggling salesman. As a character he contrasts sharply with the poor Orwell admired in reality—the colliers whose lives he documented in *The Road to Wigan Pier,* those "poor drudges underground, blackened to the eyes, with their throats full of coal dust, driving their shovels forward with arms and belly muscles of steel"(42). Gordon Comstock is a moth-eaten, threadbare little snob. He is not a victim of capitalist exploitation or business failure. He *voluntarily* descends into poverty when he quits his job in an advertising agency to become a bookseller's assistant and writer. Orwell never explains Comstock's rationale that working the same hours for half the income will somehow enhance his literary career and make him a more legitimate poet. Orwell's hero stages a kind of money-strike, which like a hunger strike must end in suicide or capitulation. When Orwell's thinly talented poet-hero decides to give up his spiteful protest, his old employer takes him back. Unlike the millions of unemployed men living on the dole in the mid-Thirties, Gordon Comstock has a job waiting for him.

Meyers, among other critics, views Gordon Comstock's character as a major flaw in the novel, noting that Comstock "lacks integrity and honour... whose envy and self-pity tend to alienate the reader's interest. He is selfish and 'horribly unfair'" (87). His battle against money is too neurotic, too self-imposed, too illogical to merit sympathy. Stansky and Abrahams share Meyer's observations:

> It is one thing to choose poverty, as a Franciscan does, to live among the poor and alleviate their suffering; it is another to do so for one's own salvation, to cleanse one's nostrils of the money-stink. There is nothing selfless in Gordon's defiance of the money-god. It is one of the peculiarities of this novel set in 1935 that its rebellious poet hero should only be fitfully aware of the hundreds of thousands of unemployed in England, living through no fault of their own below the poverty level, looking for work and unable to find it. And he is equally indifferent to any sort of political solution to the evils of the money world from which he is in flight. The Socialism espoused by his friend Ravelston... elicits from Gordon a profound boredom, a cynical No to everything Socialism claims to stand for... (123-124)

What then does Gordon and the novel represent? Stansky and Abrahams contend that in writing *Keep the Aspidistra Flying* Orwell "was exorcising a ghostly, malignant companion, the man he feared he might have become... and in doing so, liberated himself as a man and writer"(126). For his model he chose Gissing, a fellow novelist whose literary career was marked by dogged determination.

The dominant themes of Orwell's novel—the crushing effect of poverty on artistic sensibility, sex starvation, envious hatred for the literary elite, resistance to slick commercialism, and masochistic martyrdom—are drawn from *New Grub Street* in great detail.

Gordon Comstock closely parallels Gissing's hero Edwin Reardon and embodies elements of Reardon's pathetic fellow novelist, Harold Biffen, who chooses suicide over forced celibacy. In his essay on Gissing, Orwell argues that the romantic dilemma faced by these starving writers is largely a

Victorian one—that women will not choose to marry—or at least sleep with—men without hard cash:

> ... at that date the idea of delicacy, refinement, even intelligence, in the case of a woman, was hardly separable from the idea of superior social status and expensive physical surroundings. The sort of woman whom a writer would want to marry was also the sort of woman who would shrink from living in an attic. When Gissing wrote *New Grub Street* that was probably true, and it could, I think, be justly claimed that it is not true today. (*CEJL* IV 431-432)

But is was clearly true for Gordon Comstock in 1935, whose thirty-year-old virgin girl friend resolutely rebuffs his sexual advances throughout their two year relationship. By embracing poverty, Gordon only guarantees that he will suffer the loneliness of "the womanless bed" just as Gissing's Reardon loses his wife, "He had won the world's greatest prize—a woman's love—but could not retain it because his pockets were empty" (Gissing, *New* 256). Similarly, Comstock regrets the fact that he has no hold over Rosemary. "In the last resort," Orwell asks, "what holds a woman to a man, except money?" (*Keep* 103). Gissing noted that "educated girls have a pronounced distaste for London garrets; not one in fifty thousands would share poverty with the brightest genius ever born" (*New* 124). Reardon muses over the times when he was "'remote from the temptations and harassings of sexual emotion. What we call love,'" he tells Biffen, "'is mere turmoil. Who wouldn't release himself from it for ever, if the possibility offered?'" (405).

Besides the sexual torments inflicted on them by their poverty, Comstock and Reardon share an outcast's distaste for the commercially successful authors and the money world. Their resentment is personal and spiteful. It is not so much that they are critical of the system, that they wish social justice; they simply wish to exchange places:

An open carriage that passed, followed by two young girls on horseback, gave a familiar direction to Reardon's thoughts.
"If one were as rich as those people! They pass so close to us; they see us, and we see them; but the distance between us is an infinity. They don't belong to the same world as we poor wretches. They see everything in a different light; they have powers which would seem supernatural if we were suddenly endowed with them." (*New* 231)

For Gordon Comstock, the wealthy men and women rolling past him on the street appear as a people apart, a smart set who have money, luxury, and power:

Another shoal of cars swam past. One in particular caught his eye, a long slender thing, elegant as a swallow, all gleaming blue and silver; a thousand guineas it would have cost, he thought. A blue-clad chauffeur sat at the wheel, upright, immobile, like some scornful statue. At the back, in the pink-lit interior, four elegant young people, two youths, and two girls were smoking cigarettes and laughing. He had a glimpse of sleek bunny-faces; faces of ravishing pinkness and smoothness, lit by that peculiar inner glow that can never be counterfeited, the soft warm radiance of money. . . . (*Keep* 149-150)

Culture, the outcast writers perceive, lies in the access of the rich, "those moneyed young beasts from Cambridge" who "write almost in their sleep" (*Keep* 9). Both Comstock and Reardon are exiles from the literary world. Reardon's literary and romantic rival is Jasper Milvain, who denounces him as being "'the old type of unpractical artist. . . He won't make concessions. . . he can't supply the market. . . . Literature nowadays is a trade. . . . your successful man of letters is your skillful tradesman. He thinks first and foremost of the markets . . .'"(*New* 38).

Milvain is a capitalist, a cheerful tradesman providing literature for readers he values as consumers. When his friend Whelpdale suggests launching a magazine called *Chit-Chat*, Milvain becomes an enthusiastic supporter:

> "I would have the paper address itself to the quarter-educated; that is to say, the great new generation that is being turned out by the Board schools, the young men and women who can just read, but are incapable of sustained attention. People of this kind want something to occupy them in trains, and on 'buses and trams. As a rule they care for no newspapers except the Sunday ones; what they want is the lightest and frothiest of chit-chatty information—bits of stories, bits of description, bits of scandal, bits of jokes. . . .
>
> Everything must be very short, two inches at the utmost; their attention can't sustain itself beyond two inches. Even chat is too solid for them: they want chit-chat." (*New* 496-497)

Milvain's counterpart in Orwell's novel of the literary world is Comstock's wealthy Socialist friend who edits a trendy Leftist journal called *The Antichrist*. While advocating Socialism for the masses, Ravelston enjoys a high income, a plush flat, and the company of a sensuous mistress. Ravelston is a Leftist Milvain, a man of his age with his finger on the pulse of the current trend. Just as Reardon refuses to "make concessions" to the marketplace of the 1890s, Comstock resists the ideology which has captured the literary establishment of the 1930s:

> "'all this about Socialism and Capitalism and the state of the modern world and God knows what. I don't give a ---- for the state of the modern world. If the whole of England was starving except myself and people I care about, I wouldn't give a damn.'" (*Keep* 89-90)

Just as Gissing depicts Milvain as a vain, greedy capitalist without taste or insight who apes the manner of publishing barons, Orwell describes Ravelston as the kind of effete pseudo-revolutionary who is totally out of touch with social and political realities:

> You could tell him at a glance for a rich young man. He wore the uniform of the moneyed intelligentsia; an old tweed coat—but it was one of those coats which have been made by a good tailor and grow more aristocratic as they grow older—very loose grey flannel bags, a

grey pullover, much-worn brown shoes. He made a point of going every-where, even to fashionable houses and expensive restaurants, in these clothes, just to show his contempt for upper-class conventions; he did not fully realise that it is only the upper classes who can do these things. (80-81)

Comstock and Reardon follow a common downward path, refusing to compromise to literary convention. Reardon toils on his novel despite depression, writer's block, and financial ruin. Poverty forces him to separate from his wife, sell his books and furnishings at a loss, and leave his flat. Glancing at the empty apartment, he feels totally isolated, "He felt utterly alone in the world . . . These stripped rooms were symbolical of his life; losing money, he had lost everything. . . . Love is one of the first things to be frightened away poverty" (*New* 289). Desperate for income, he abandons writing as a pretense and accepts a menial job, "Let the man of letters be forgotten; he was seeking for remunerative employment, just as if he had never written a line" (*New* 293). Accepting employment in a hospital, Reardon was "back once more in the days of no reputation, a harmless clerk, a decent wage-earner" (*New* 293). Reardon then falls deeper into poverty:

> He kept one suit of clothes for his hours of attendance at the hospital. . . . That which he wore at home and in his street wanderings declared poverty at every point. . . In his present state of mind he cared nothing how disreputable he looked to passers-by. These seedy habiliments were the tokens of his degradation, and at times he regarded them...with pleasurable contempt. . . . he defiantly took a place among the miserables of the nether world, and nursed hatred of all who were well-to-do. (377)

Gissing points out that Reardon almost savors his suffering because "misery magnifies him in own estimate" (*New* 373), feeding his ego, "An extraordinary arrogance now and then possessed him; he stood amid his poor surroundings with the sensations of an outraged exile, and laughed aloud in furious contempt of all who censured or pitied him" (*New* 373). As Reardon sinks deeper into poverty, his wife inherits ten thousand pounds, but Reardon refuses to accept assistance from her. His poverty, symbolized by a threadbare overcoat, shames him to the point that it prevents him from meeting his wife for an attempted reconciliation. Amy Reardon cannot tolerate her husband's shabbiness. However, when their son is diagnosed with diphtheria, she summons Reardon. Despite a severe cold, Reardon races to his son's bedside. The child dies, and Reardon, weakened by exposure to the elements, falls seriously ill and dies.

Amy Reardon leads another "impractical" writer to an early death. Poor, sex-starved Harold Biffen visits her to pay respects to his friend's widow. But this visit turns Biffen's long smoldering unrequited love into a flaming passion, ". . .after that hour of intimate speech with Amy, he never again knew rest of mind or heart" (*New* 523). In his loneliness, the wealthy widow becomes an unobtainable goddess, representing "all that is lovely in womanhood; to his starved soul and senses she was woman, the complement of his frustrate being" (*New* 526). Lonely, frustrated beyond measure, Biffen cannot "bear to walk the streets where the faces of beautiful women would encounter him" (*New* 526). Leaving his house, he chooses to travel narrow slum streets to no relief:

> Yet even here he was too often reminded that the poverty-stricken of the class to which poverty is natural were not condemned to endure in solitude. Only he who belonged to no class, who was rejected alike by his fellows in privation and by his equals in intellect, must die without having known the touch of a loving woman's hand. (*New* 526)

Depressed, running out of funds and unable to write, Biffen seeks peace in death. Purchasing poison, he heads to a park to take his life. He thinks of Reardon, "but of Amy he thought only as of that star which had just come into his vision above the edge of dark foliage—beautiful, but infinitely remote" (*New* 529).

At novel's end Amy, the prize, is won by "practical" Jasper Milvain. Amy and Milvain agree that the "world is a glorious place—for rich people" (*New* 550-551).

Perhaps aware that his readers would find the masochism and self-destructive spite of Reardon and Biffen difficult to accept, Gissing came to their defense, opening a chapter with a direct appeal on his characters' behalf:

> The chances are that you have neither under-standing nor sympathy for men such as Edwin Reardon and Harold Biffen. They merely provoke you. They seem to you inert, flabby, weakly envious, foolishly obstinate, impiously mutinous, and many other things. You are made angrily contemptuous by their failure to get on; why don't they bestir themselves, push and bustle. . . in short, take a leaf from the book of Mr Jasper Milvain?
>
> But try to imagine a personality wholly unfitted for the rough and tumble of the world's labour-market. . . You scorn their passivity; but it was their nature and their merit to be passive. Gifted with independent means, each of them would have taken quite a different aspect in your eyes. The sum of their faults was their inability to earn money; but, indeed, that inability does not call for unmingled disdain.
>
> (*New* 462)

In chronicling the downward spiral of Gordon Comstock, Orwell drew on key elements of Reardon and Biffen. Orwell, however, did not defend his protagonist, repeatedly demonstrating that Gordon Comstock is passive, spiteful, and masochistic. His money problems are wholly self-imposed. Unlike Reardon, he voluntarily exchanges a four-pound-a-week job for a two-pound-a-week job in an illogical attempt to free himself from money. While Gissing wove several characters into his plot, depicting an entire class of struggling literary workers in a modern Grub Street, Orwell offers readers only Gordon, a smug rebel. His demise is hastened

48 ART AND CASH

not by environmental forces beyond his control, but by his own self-destructive actions. Having received fifty dollars from an American magazine for a poem, Comstock goes on a spree, wasting money on overpriced food and drinks. Flush with cash, he selects a predatory-looking tart and heads to a brothel. In a comic scene he is unable to achieve the sexual gratification he craves. Impotent from drink, he collapses to the floor, sucking from a bottle like an infant. The next morning he awakes in a jail cell to discover that he has been arrested for disorderly conduct, his sexual crime exposed—a purely Gissing touch. Gordon is fired and evicted by his prudish landlady. Taking a drudge job for survival, Gordon moves into a slum garret and allows himself "to go to pieces." His girl friend Rosemary arrives to rescue him, offering her body. Their single joyless union leads to pregnancy, forcing Gordon to "do the right thing." Accepting responsibilities, he terminates his money-strike, returns to the advertising agency, abandons his literary career, and becomes what he—and Orwell—always despised, a little man in a little job.

The texture of *Keep the Aspidistra Flying* is woven with scenes drawn from *New Grub Street*. There is the same focus on dark streets, shabby clothing, cold rooms, and tasteless meals. Reardon suffers with his one decent suit and threadbare topcoat. Gordon's best suit is three years old, and he must take care to hide the torn spot on his necktie (*Keep* 63). Like Reardon, Comstock endures soul-crushing loneliness—"That is the devilish thing about poverty, the ever-recurrent thing—loneliness. Day after day with never an intelligent person to talk to; night after night back to your godless room, always alone" (*Keep* 64). Like Reardon, Comstock moves downward, exchanging inexpensive lodgings with pretensions of middle class decency for an outright slum. And like Reardon, Gordon comes to savor poverty out of spite, almost anxious to descend into Gissing's "nether world":

> He liked to think about the lost people, the under ground people, tramps, beggars, criminals, prostitutes. It is a good world that they inhabit, down there in their frowzy kips and spikes. He liked to think that beneath the world of money there is that great sluttish underworld where failure and success have no meaning; a sort of kingdom of ghosts where all are equal. That was where he wished to be, down in the ghost kingdom, *below* ambition. It comforted him somehow to think of the smoke-dim slums of South London sprawling on and on, a huge graceless wilderness where you could lose yourself forever.
> (*Keep* 203-204)

Comstock goes without washing or shaving and refuses to clean his room, allowing it to become dusty and cluttered with dirty dishes. He relishes this squalor, "Without regret, almost intentionally, he was letting himself go to pieces" (*Keep* 208). His incomplete cycle of poems, *London Pleasures*, is the only thing that symbolizes his rebellion against the conformity and conventionality of the money world. Comstock clings to his poetry as a shield against becoming "a typical little bowler-hatted sneak... the little docile cit who slips home by the six-fifteen to a supper of cottage pie and stewed tinned pears, half an hour's listening-in to the B.B.C. Symphony Concert, and then perhaps a spot of licit sexual intercourse if his wife 'feels in the mood!' What a fate!"(*Keep* 48).

But after impregnating Rosemary, Gordon chucks *London Pleasures* down a sewer, abandoning his writing career as did Reardon. Instead of suicide, Comstock surrenders. He takes a job writing ads for foot deodorant, marries, and moves into a modest flat overlooking Paddington Station.

Orwell concentrates on the sheer drudgery of writing, demonstrating how a frustrated and exhausted Comstock struggles over each line. His two years' labor *London Pleasures* is described as "that labyrinthine mess of words! And tonight's achievement—two lines crossed out; two lines backward instead of forward" (*Keep* 34-35).

In an essay about Gissing, Orwell focused on those scenes in *New Grub Street* depicting Reardon agonizing over how many pages he must fill in a day to survive as a hack writer. Orwell noted how Reardon's torment is exacerbated when his wife counts the pages:

> His wife, of course, has not the faintest under-standing of what is meant by literary creation. There is a terrible passage—terrible, at least, to anyone who earns his living by writing—in which she calculates the number of pages that it would be possible to write in a day, and hence the number of novels that her husband may be expected to produce in a year. . . .(*CEJL* IV 432)

The drudgery of writing leads one character in *New Grub Street* to imagine a literary machine, not unlike the novel writing machine Orwell describes in *Nineteen Eighty-Four:*

> A few days ago her startled eye had caught an advertisement in the newspaper, headed "Literary Machine"; had it then been invented at last, some automaton to supply the place of such poor creatures as herself, to turn out books and articles? Alas! The machine was only one for holding volumes. . . But surely before long some Edison would make the true automaton; the problem must be comparatively such a simple one. Only to throw in a given number of old books, and have them reduced, blended, modernised into a single one for today's consumption. (*New* 138)

Orwell emphasized Gissing's theme of sexual starvation in his tale of literary and personal frustration. Like Harold Biffen, Gordon Comstock curses his forced celibacy. Like Biffen, he believes himself uniquely singled out for a sexless existence. Educated, decent women will have nothing to do with a "moth-eaten" clerk with literary pretensions. Comstock shares Biffen's observation that the poor are different. He celebrates their unrestrained sexual impulses, declaring, "Hats off to the factory lad who with fourpence in the world puts his girl in the family way! At least he's got blood and not money in his veins"(*Keep* 44).

For Comstock women who pass him on the street are painful reminders of his loneliness, his desperate need for "the touch of a loving woman's hand":

> How damned unfair it is that we are filled to the brim with these tormenting desires and then forbidden to satisfy them! Why should one, merely because one has no money, be deprived of *that*? . . . . As he walked down the dark street . . . there was a strangely hopeful feeling in his breast. He half-believed that somewhere ahead in the darkness a woman's body was waiting for him. But also he knew that no woman was waiting, not even Rosemary. (*Keep* 103)

As he approaches women in the street, Comstock senses immediate rejection, "None had eyes for Gordon. He walked among them as though invisible, save that their bodies avoided him when he passed them" (*Keep* 105).

The spirit of Comstock's muddled and self-inflicted suffering echoes Orwell's later observation about Gissing and his times: "Money and women were therefore the two instruments through which society avenged itself on the courageous and the intelligent" (*CEJL* IV 430). Orwell, who had difficulty in writing about female characters, relied heavily on Gissing's ability to capture the painful complexities of human sexuality.

FIVE
THE WOMAN BUSINESS

> In his treatment of sexual matters Gissing is surprisingly frank, considering the time at which he was writing. It is not that he writes pornography or expresses approval of sexual promiscuity, but simply that he is willing to face the facts.
>
> George Orwell

The "facts" Orwell forced his protagonists to face were not pleasant: sexual frustration, loneliness, demeaning fornications with prostitutes, botched love affairs, and loveless marriages. Irritated by his three year sexless relationship with Rosemary and infrequent "squalid" dealings with tarts, Gordon Comstock curses his sexual desires, "This woman business! What a bore it is! What a pity we can't cut it right out, or at least be like the animals—minutes of ferocious lust and months of icy chastity"(*Keep* 102). Winston Smith, separated from a frigid wife, curses the fact that his sex life is limited to "filthy scuffles at intervals of years." His sexual frustration boils over into pure sadism during the Two Minutes Hate as he transfers his anger toward a young woman:

> Vivid, beautiful hallucinations flashed through his mind. He would flog her to death with a rubber truncheon. He would tie her naked to a stake and shoot her full of arrows like Saint Sebastian. He would ravish her and cut her throat at the moment of climax. Better than before, moreover, he realized *why* it was that he hated her. He hated her because she was young and pretty and sexless, because he wanted to go to bed with her and would never do so, because round her sweet supple waist, which seemed to ask you to encircle it with your arm, there was only the odious scarlet sash, aggressive symbol of chastity.
>
> (*1984* 16-17)

George Bowling, badgered by a nagging wife, contemplates a weekend with a tart, lamenting that "no woman will look at him unless paid to."

Orwell depicted capitalist society as largely anti-sexual, at least for those with middle-class pretensions and no cash. Gordon's and Rosemary's relationship is frustrated because their respective landladies discourage visitors of the opposite sex. Comstock's landlady views women as "plague rats." In creating his nightmare Utopia, Orwell exacerbated Victorian prudery into Stalinist terror so that in *Nineteen Eighty-Four* the Party would deny marriage to any couple showing signs of physical attraction. "Sexual intercourse," Orwell stated, "was to be looked on as a slightly disgusting minor operation, like having an enema" (*1984* 57). Sex then becomes a "political act," an act of rebellion against Big Brother—like the factory lad protesting the money god by impregnating his girl friend.

Orwell's interest in Gissing rests in part because Gissing was willing to address the true sexual nature of human experience. In reading the details of Gissing's personal life and early tragedy, Orwell noted an affinity with his own experiences. Like Gissing, Orwell had endured embarrassment and exploitation. He once told Mabel Fierz, a personal friend, of an early affair he had as a young writer in Paris:

In fact, on the question of girls, he once said that of all the girls he'd known before he met his wife, the one he loved best was a little trollop he'd picked up in a cafe in Paris. She was beautiful, and had a figure like a boy, an Eton crop and in every way desirable. Anyway, he had a relationship with this girl for some time and came a point one day he came back to his room, and this paragon had decamped with everything he possessed. All his luggage and his money and everything (qtd Crick 121).

Orwell's early sexual encounters may have paralleled Gissing's, as evidenced by the cynical poem he wrote about his experiences in Burma:

ROMANCE

When I was young and had no sense
    In far-off Mandalay
I lost my heart to a Burmese girl
    As lovely as the day.

Her skin was gold; her hair was jet
    Her teeth were ivory;
I said "For twenty silver pieces,
    Maiden, sleep with me."

She looked at me, so pure, so sad,
    The loveliest thing alive,
And in her lisping, virgin voice,
    Stood out for twenty-five.

(qtd Crick 93)

Orwell's novels mirror Gissing's preoccupation with "ladylike and unladylike women." The sexual politics of *Burmese Days* are identical to those of *Workers in the Dawn*. Both of these first novels end with the protagonists committing suicide after losing the opportunity for a life-saving, soul-sustaining relationship with an idealized woman.

The plots of both novels are largely driven by the protagonist's tormenting Madonna-whore crisis. In both novels a secret sexual relationship with an unacceptable woman is exposed, shattering any possibility of marriage with an intellectually compatible woman.

Gissing's artist hero, Arthur Golding, leaves the home of his benefactor for the London slums where he flirts with revolutionary politics. There he encounters Carrie Mitchell, a girl of the streets who has been impregnated and abandoned by a "gentleman." Golding rescues her, marries her, and hopes to reform her. But Carrie, like Gissing's own wife, refuses to be reshaped in her husband's image. Though described as "sensual," Carrie is selfish, impudent, and brash. She continues to drink, invites whore friends to their lodgings, and steals. At one point Carrie and her landlady conspire to kill Golding for his inheritance. Gissing portrays Golding's motivations as largely idealistic, though it is obvious that her behavior is meant to be viewed as a punishment for his sexual folly, his naive hope of discovering the proverbial "whore with a heart of gold."

John Flory, the timber merchant hero of *Burmese Days*, finds his lonely outpost tolerable because of gin and the company of a Burmese mistress, Ma Hla May. Flory purchased her from her parents for three hundred rupees. Orwell describes her as being a "doll" or a "kitten," an almost inhuman, alien sex toy. Ma Hla May was, Orwell writes, "like a doll. . . an outlandish doll and yet a grotesquely beautiful one"(*Burmese Days* 41). She excites Flory's sexual appetite, but immediately after intercourse Ma Hla May appears "nauseating and dreadful to him" (49). After she has served her purpose, Flory's shame and self-disgust lead him to become abusive and dismissive. In return, Ma Hla May wheedles money out of him and steals.

Golding's wife contrasts sharply with his intellectual equal, Helen Norman, his benefactor's daughter. An intelligent woman educated in Germany, she is Gissing's ideal. Several chapters of the novel are devoted to her university diary, detailing her intellectual development. A reformer, Helen dedicates her life to aiding the poor. To Gissing's sensitive hero, Helen is an angelic beauty, a literal Madonna figure:

> . . . for him her beauty was something absolute, a type of perfection which, in the nature of things, could not be compared with other types.
> . . . He gazed at her till an actual halo, a visible aureola, seemed to glitter about her, and he feared to turn away his eyes for a moment lest the beautiful effect should vanish. . . .
> . . .Even as a vision of the sweet-faced Madonna may have floated before the eyes of Fra Angelico. . .
> so Arthur sat, brush in hand. . . unable to think of anything but the chaste features of Helen Norman. . . (*Workers* I 313-314)

Helen becomes "his Muse, his tutelary goddess" (*Workers* I 315). Golding lovingly sketches his ideal woman whose cold, classic beauty embodies purity and chastity.

Carrie, on the other hand, possesses a beauty "of a somewhat sensual type" that exudes sexuality. She "excites" Golding's "natural ardor." After their disastrous marriage, Carrie discovers Golding's idealized portrait of Helen and confronts him in a jealous rage. Smiling with "angry scorn," she taunts Golding with the picture. Gissing's hero suffers intensely as Carrie, crude and sexual, ridicules his feminine ideal, "It was torture to him to see her sneering at the picture; it was desecration for it to remain in her hands" (*Workers* II 161). Suspecting a romantic rival, Carrie insists Golding destroy the picture. When he hesitates, she angrily tears it in two.

Golding agonizingly contemplates his conflict in the Madonna-whore dichotomy:

> Helen and Carrie! Oh God! How could he bear to reflect upon the two together? In these moments every lovable look which he had ever seen on Helen's face . . . was as real to him as if he had been subject to its influence but a moment ago. What a spirit of sweet and noble

> intelligence breathed from her whole person. Intelligence—intelligence! That, after all, was what Arthur most worshipped in her...
>
> ...But poor Carrie—alas! What was all her outward beauty when she utterly lacked all traces of that divine fire.... Who was this that he had married? What beast's nature encased in a human form?
> (*Workers* II 164)

Wrestling with this dilemma, Golding walks through the London streets, noticing the prostitutes. "How hideous were most of them!" he thinks, yet finds his "passions were awakened" by the "novel sensation of witnessing such scenes" (*Workers* II 165). He follows a "dainty" *fille perdue* "without thinking" but backs off when she turns to address him. Heading home, he discovers Carrie in the midst of a street brawl, her clothes in shreds. Golding rescues her and drags her to their "cheerless" room, which Carrie's breath fills "with the smell of spirits" (*Workers* II 167).

In *Burmese Days,* John Flory's desire for an intelligent companion is inflamed with the arrival of Elizabeth Lackersteen, the only available white female in the small European community. At twenty-two with stylishly short hair, Elizabeth, fresh from Paris, represents everything Flory has long felt exiled from—art, intelligent conversation, Western civilization, youth, and decency. On first meeting Elizabeth, Flory plunges into an excited literary conversation. Immediately, they are confronted by Ma Hla May. The two women regard his other with suspicious curiosity, and the Madonna-whore delineations are sharply drawn:

> No contrast could have been stranger; the one faintly colored as an apple blossom, the other dark and garish with a gleam almost metallic on her cylinder of ebony hair and the salmon-pink silk of her *longyi*. Flory thought he had never noticed before how dark Ma Hla May's face was, and how outlandish her tiny, stiff body, straight as a soldier's, with not a curve in it except the vase-like curve of her hips... For the best part of a minute neither of them could take her eyes from the other; but which found the spectacle more grotesque, more incredible, there is

no saying. (*Burmese Days* 76)

Flory attempts to dismiss Ma Hla May as a servant, telling the naive Elizabeth that she is a laundress. Elizabeth accepts Flory's story, remarking, "Oh, is *that* what Burmese women are like? They *are* queer little creatures! I saw a lot of them on my way up here in the train, but do you know, I thought they were all boys. They're just like a kind of Dutch doll, aren't they?" (76). Throughout the scene, Flory endures the agonizing fear that his mistress will cause a scene, comforting himself with the fact that neither woman speaks the other's language.

Like Golding, Flory seeks to escape the clutches of a socially inferior sexual partner. But Ma Hla May, like Carrie, refuses to let go. Ma Hla May becomes jealous, threatening Flory's attempt to rehabilitate himself to become a suitable marriage prospect for Elizabeth.

Both Golding and Flory come to see a union with an idealized intellectual woman as an avenue to a higher form of existence, an escape from triviality, isolation, and the mediocre tedium of common life. Both come to declare their love. Golding sends Helen a letter, stating, "'The passion with which I thus offer you my soul has made my hands tremble and my mind fail'"(*Workers* III 313). Golding tells Helen of his need for intellectual companionship and a relationship above that possible with "ordinary women." Helen returns his love; Golding is elated—until Carrie returns. She embraces him and Golding pulls back, "lest his hand, fresh from the clasp of Helen's, should be soiled by the mere touch of hers" (*Workers* III 328). Similarly, Flory approaches Elizabeth, seeking rescue from his loneliness. "'This country's been a kind of solitary hell to me,'" he confesses to her, "'. . . and yet I tell you it could be paradise if one weren't alone'" (*Burmese Days* 153). Flory's proposal is interrupted by an earthquake, and he is soon temporarily eclipsed in Elizabeth's eyes by the arrival of a virile young officer. Though smug and narrow-minded, Lieutenant Verrall is a far better match for Elizabeth than a middle-aged timber merchant. Spotting the two words "the Honourable" next to Verrall's name, Elizabeth's aunt dissuades her niece's interest in Flory by informing her that he is "keeping a Burmese woman." Disgusted, Elizabeth rejects Flory and rides and dances with Verrall. Burning with envy, Flory is tormented, "The vision of Elizabeth in Verrall's arms haunted him like a neuralgia or an earache" (*Burmese Days* 192).

But the "honourable" officer on temporary duty is apparently not interested in marriage, leading Elizabeth's aunt to reluctantly endorse Flory as a second choice. Flory's heroic actions during a native insurrection lead Elizabeth to view him more favorably. When young Verrall suddenly decamps, leaving a train of disgruntled native creditors at the station, Flory becomes Elizabeth's sole prospect. But as with Arthur Golding, John Flory cannot free himself from his past.

Both *Workers in the Dawn* and *Burmese Days* feature nightmare scenes of sexual guilt discovered. After Golding declares his love to Helen, a drunken Carrie arrives at the door of her friends, exposing their marriage:

> "Arthur Golding!" she cried, glaring round the room out of bloodshot eyes in a manner more like a maniac than one merely drunk. "I want Arthur Golding. . . . I want my husband." (*Workers* III 344)

Orwell heightens the humiliation by having a direct confrontation between whore and Madonna occur in church. Flory's young officer rival has fled, leaving him free to pursue Elizabeth. Attending church, Flory plans to propose immediately after the service. His musings of married life are interrupted when Ma Hla May arrives, shrieking:

> "*Pike-san pay-like! Pike-san pay-like!*"
> Everyone jumped in their seats and turned round. It was Ma Hla May. As they turned she stepped inside the church. . .

> ". . . Flory, Flory! . . . . That one sitting in front there. . . . Turn round and face me, you coward! Where is the money you promised me?"
>
> She was shrieking like a maniac. The people gaped at her, too astounded to move or speak. Her face was grey with powder, her greasy hair was tumbling down, her *longyi* was ragged at the bottom. She looked like a screaming hag of the bazaar. Flory's bowels seemed to have turned to ice. Oh, God, God! Must they know—must Elizabeth know — that *that* was the woman who had been his mistress? But there was not a hope, not the vestige of a hope, of any mistake. . . . The wretched woman was yelling out a detailed account of what Flory had done to her.
>
> "Look at me, you white men, and you women, too, look at me! Look how he has ruined me! . . . . Turn round and look at me! Look at this body that you have kissed a thousand times—look—" She began actually to tear her clothes open. . ." (*Burmese Days* 231-232)

Golding and Flory are forced to admit their sexual sins to their idealized Madonna-figures. Soiled in their presence, they beg understanding and offer excuses. Golding attempts to explain to Helen that Carrie was never actually his wife:

> "She was never really my wife, for I never truly loved her. What right has she to come and put forward such a claim . . . . My wife?—This degraded, horrible, brutalised creature to call herself my wife! If the word means anything at all, it is you, Helen, to whom it should apply. Yes, you are indeed my wife, have been my wife from the moment when our lips first met. . . . The law may recognize that other one as my wife; but I, never—never!" (*Workers* III 358-359)

Although sympathetic to Golding's plight, Helen urges him to honor his duty to his wife, stating, "'I was no good angel to you when my image induced you to shut your ears to the voice of conscience and let your wife once more go her way,'" (*Workers* III 359). He begs her not to renounce him, telling Helen, "'Better bid me end my life at once, for what use will there be in living?'" (359). But Helen insists he respect his marriage vows, "'How can you, who have been so strongly impressed with the sufferings inflicted by society upon the poor and outcast, permit yourself to altogether forget this wretched woman, careless of what becomes of her?'" (361).

Golding nevertheless attempts to buy Carrie off, making financial provisions for her before leaving for exile in America. A letter reaches him in upstate New York, informing him Carrie is near death from her "dissipated life." The news offers Golding a chance of freedom, an opportunity to honestly reclaim Helen. But the mail also contains an English newspaper which includes Helen Norman's obituary. Golding is driven to despair, "In her person the ideal of his life had perished. . . . Why should he live?"

Faced with the prospect of a life alone, Golding feels like a "wrecked and manless ship upon an ebbing sea" (*Workers* III 435). Shouting Helen's name, Golding throws himself over Niagara Falls.

Flory's sexual sin has racial elements. Elizabeth's distaste for Asians is well pronounced and Flory's sexual relationship with a prostitute is doubly repulsive to her because the woman is Burmese. Flory, like Golding, pleads forgiveness and begs her to save him from "a sort of death-in-life!" Flory tells her of his loneliness and states that she is "'the sole person on earth who could save me from it'" (*Burmese Days* 235). Grasping for some way to win her companionship at any cost, he offers a platonic marriage, "'If you like, I'd marry you and promise never even to touch you with my finger. . . . But I can't go on with my life alone, always alone. Can't you bring yourself ever to forgive me?'" (235). But Elizabeth, detesting him even more for his self-pity and weakness, refuses, stating coldly, "'I wouldn't marry you if you were the last man on earth"(235). Facing the prospect of a life without Elizabeth, Flory returns to his home and shoots himself through the heart.

The Madonna-whore theme run throughout Gissing's and Orwell's novels, tormenting their heroes. The idealized lover is chaste and intelligent and therefore critical of suitors. The whore is available for a price, but sexual satisfaction is tempered by humiliation, guilt, fear of exposure, and blackmail.

As in Gissing's novels, Orwell's plots frequently turn on sexual matters. John Flory is a sexual suicide. Gordon Comstock is prompted to terminate his rebellious money-strike when he impregnates Rosemary and is forced to marry. In *A Clergyman's Daughter* the clumsy advances of a middle-aged lecher unhinge the mind of Dorothy Hare, Orwell's only female protagonist, and drive the twenty-seven year old virgin to wander London in an amnesiac daze. George Bowling, the obese husband in *Coming Up for Air*, accepts the painful realities of living on the brink of world war in terms of tolerating a jealous wife. A sexual relationship with Julia inspires Winston Smith to actively rebel against Big Brother. In breaking him in the dreaded Room 101, the party forces him to betray his lover.

For Orwell women are a problem, a necessary complication to life. His protagonists regard female companionship the way addicts view narcotics—an expensive and elusive compulsion. In all of Orwell's fiction there are two males who appear sexually satisfied.

Ravelston, Gordon Comstock's wealthy Socialist friend, enjoys a relationship with Hermione, rich, sensual, willing. Hermione has no interest in marriage, which she regards as being "too much fag" (*Keep* 93). She can afford to violate the strict propriety of middle-class morality. Yet even Hermione, like an addictive drug, has dangerous side effects. Orwell views her as a sexual animal with no intellectual interests or political sensitivity, "Whenever there was nothing particular to do, Hermione always fell asleep as promptly as an animal" (*Keep* 96). She is a "sleepy siren" who lures Ravelston to abandon his Socialist values, "The woman-scent breathed out of her, a powerful wordless propaganda against all altruism and all justice" (98). Ravelston savors sex with her with the same liberal guilt he feels entering a posh restaurant. Winston Smith encounters Julia, a middle-aged man's dream girl. Young, promiscuous, brash, she represents a woman gifted with a male sex drive, enjoying relations with no concerns of security, decency, or commitment. Julia briefly rescues Smith from his life of sexual frustration and humiliation. But like Hermione, she too, is always falling asleep when Winston attempts to discuss politics. She, too, breaks the rules like an animal out of selfishness not political ideology. Winston, though enlivened by her sexuality, tells Julia, "'You're only a rebel from the waist downwards...'"(*1984* 129).

For the rest of Orwell's male characters, sexual needs are met with half measures, particularly prostitution. Before purchasing Ma Hla May, John Flory, slept with "aged Jewish whores with the faces of crocodiles" (*Burmese Days* 58). Gordon Comstock had been with tarts, but "even when they were not tarts it had been squalid, always squalid" (*Keep* 104). George Bowling sadly reflects that no woman will look at him "unless paid to." Winston Smith's diary opens with his recollection of an encounter with a two-dollar whore, a fifty-year-old hag in a bug-ridden cellar. Despite the filth, her toothless smile, Winston states, "'I went ahead and did it just the same'" (*1984* 60). Like all of Orwell's characters, Smith finds sexual satisfaction only in "filthy scuffles at intervals of years" (59).

As in Gissing's novels, Orwell's characters live in a society depicted as grimly anti-sexual—unless one has the means to live comfortably outside the social norm. Reardon's marriage is destroyed by poverty. A threadbare coat, his inability to maintain a decent apartment emasculates him in his wife's eyes and she cannot bring herself to love him. Gordon Comstock sees his relationship with Rosemary limited to platonic hand-holding because he lacks financial stability. "'You won't sleep with me,'" he tells her, "'simply and solely because I've got no money. . . .And if I had a decent income you'd go to bed with me to-morrow. . . . you've got that deep-down mystical feeling that somehow a man without money isn't worthy of you. He's a weakling, a sort of half-man—that's how you feel'"(*Keep* 114).

Although Orwell and Gissing despair that intelligent women are hard to find, they also characterize educated women as less than desirable partners. Intellectual women are invariably frigid in their novels. "The truly emancipated woman—it was Godwin's opinion," Gissing states of his *Born in Exile* hero, "is almost always asexual; to him, therefore, utterly repugnant" (*Born* 247). Learning of Rosemary's pregnancy, Gordon Comstock enters a library seeking information on childbirth and encounters a female librarian, a "university graduate, young, colourless, spectacled and intensely disagreeable" (*Keep* 231-232). Convinced no male "ever consulted works of reference except in search of pornography," she interrogates Comstock before reluctantly turning over medical books (232). As he studied, Gordon "could feel her pince-nez probing the back of his neck at long range, trying to decide from his demeanor whether he was really searching for information or merely picking out the dirty bits" (233).

Above all, it is Orwell's depiction of marriage that matches so directly with Gissing's outlook. Orwell's two married protagonists—Winston Smith and George Bowling—both contemplate homicide shortly after marriage. Seeking escape from his frigid robot spouse, Smith recalls the impulse to push his wife from a cliff just three months after their marriage. For Bowling, wife-murder was "a kind of fantasy that one enjoys thinking about" (*Coming* 158-159). Actual murder was out of the question. "Besides," he notes, "chaps who murder their wives always get copped. . . . When a woman's bumped off, her husband is always the first suspect—which gives you a little side-glimpse of what people really think about marriage" (159). Bowling views marriage as a dismal trap:

> What really gets me down is the dreary attitude toward life that it implies. If marriage was just an open swindle—if the woman trapped you into it and then turned round and said, "Now, you bastard, I've caught you and you're going to work for me while I have a good time"—I wouldn't mind it so much. (*Coming* 159)

Although mourning his "womanless" bed, Gordon Comstock views marriage as a "trap":

> Marriage is only a trap set for you by the money-god. You grab the bait; snap goes the trap; and there you are, chained by the leg to some "good" job till they cart you to Kensal Green. And what a life! Licit sexual intercourse in the shade of the aspidistra. Pram pushing and sneaky adulteries. And the wife finding you out and breaking the cut-glass whisky decanter over your head. (*Keep* 104)

These attitudes greatly match Gissing's depictions of joyless marriages. Happiness in marriage, the protagonist of *The Whirlpool* considers, is best measured by the lack of pain rather than the degree of pleasure. "Happiness in marriage is a term of such vague application," he reasons (335). Perhaps only one in 10,000 marriages is happy he realizes. In Gissing's novel *In the Year of the Jubilee,* Lionel Tarrant tells his wife, "'There is not one wife in fifty thousand who retains her husband's love after the first year of marriage'" (373). The only couples who are happy, he argues, "'are those who are rich enough, and sensible enough, to have two distinct establishments under the same roof. The ordinary eight or ten-roomed house, inhabited by decent middle-class folk, is a gruesome sight. What a huddlement of male and female!'" (374). Escaping such a "huddlement," a character in the same novel relishes his separation from his wife:

> He was a free man. No snarl greeted him as he turned his head upon the pillow; he could lie and meditate, could rise quietly when the moment sounded, could go downstairs for a leisurely meal . . . Simple, elementary pleasures, but how he savoured them after his years of

sordid bondage! (345)

Orwell was attracted to Gissing's honesty in dealing with sexual matters, particularly in depicting the sexual starvation of sensitive men without the money and confidence to win a woman's love.

Unlike Gissing, Orwell did not create memorable, or even realistic female characters. In developing his only novel with a female protagonist, *A Clergyman's Daughter*, Orwell closely relied on Gissing's treatment of women, particularly in *The Odd Women*, the work Orwell considered one of the best novels in English.

SIX
THE RAGGED REGIMENT: *A CLERGYMAN'S DAUGHTER* AND *THE ODD WOMEN*

> "Don't lose *The Odd Women,* will you."
> George Orwell, letter
> to Richard Rees

In developing his least satisfying novel and his only work featuring a female protagonist, Orwell sought guidance from Gissing's treatment of women. *The Odd Women,* Gissing's pioneer novel about women's lives, was one of Orwell's favorite books. He mourned however that the novel was by 1948 "about as thoroughly out of print as a book can be" (*CEJL* IV 429). "I possess a copy myself," he told readers, "in one of those nasty red-covered cheap editions that flourished before the 1914 war, but that is the only copy I have ever seen or heard of" (IV 429). Nevertheless, this obscure novel, which he considered one of the best in the English language, provided him with an influential model.

Orwell never created credible female characters. His women never achieve full personalities. Rather, they generally appear as representatives of a stereotype—nagging wife, sluttish workgirl, predatory tart, frigid intellectual. In Orwell's fiction, women are creatures, offering or withholding their sexuality, providing release or torment to his male characters. In creating Dorothy Hare, Orwell had to invent a feminine consciousness. Here his writing failed him. Dorothy is the least life-like, the least believable of his eccentric protagonists.

In a novel exploring the loss of religious faith, Orwell chooses as his central character not a minister's enlightened battle with agnosticism, but his daughter's. At twenty-seven, Dorothy practices a Sunday-school kind of faith devoted to charity and rigid self-denial. She keeps house for her father, runs errands, and devotes her time to small town church work—sick calls, rummage sales, Sunday school. Whenever selfish thoughts enter her mind, she pricks herself with a needle. The most distinguishing aspect of her personality is her absolute horror of sexual activity, which she euphemistically denounces as "all that."

She has a pathological fear of men:

> To be kissed or fondled by a man—to feel heavy male arms about her and thick male lips bearing down upon her own—was terrifying and repulsive to her . . . .
>
> If only they would leave you *alone!* she thought. . . . Why did they always have to kiss you and maul you about? They were dreadful when they kissed you—dreadful and a little disgusting, like some large, furry beast that rubs itself against you, all too friendly and yet liable to turn dangerous at an moment. And beyond their kissing and mauling there lay always the suggestion of those other, monstrous things . . . of which she could hardly even bear to think. (*Clergyman's* 91-92)

Attempting to explain the cause of her frigidity, Orwell offers a clumsy description of a childhood memory of seeing her parents engaging in intercourse. These "dreadful scenes" scarred her, leaving in Orwell's words "a deep, secret wound in her mind" (*Clergyman's* 93). Later frightened by a steel engraving of a satyr, she came to associate all men with evil rapacious satyrs, so that "Nothing would ever overcome her horror of *all that...*"(93). She rejects the marriage proposal of a young curate because even marriage to a clergyman would entail intercourse so "of course she had had to say No" (93). This extreme aversion to sex Orwell offhandedly notes is ". . . moreover, a thing too common nowadays, among educated women, to occasion any kind of surprise" (94).

The stilted psychology of the novel is furthered by the use of amnesia as a plot device. The sexual overtures of the town lecher, Mr. Warburton (named after the hero of Gissing's last novel, *Will Warburton*) help to unhinge Dorothy's mind so that she falls asleep and awakens weeks later walking the streets of London inexplicably dressed like a cheap tart. Slowly regaining consciousness, she recognizes her surroundings, then slowly discovers that she exists, wondering, "'Am I a man or a woman?'" Touching her body, "her hands encountered breasts. She was a woman, therefore. Only women had breasts" (98).

Unable to remember her father or her home town of Knype Hill, Dorothy is taken in by drifters and migrants. She works as a hop picker, then obtains a teaching position in a small private girls' school operated by a greedy, mean-spirited crone named Mrs. Creevy. Dorothy is appalled by the total ignorance of the students and labors to develop innovative teaching methods. But her efforts are short-lived. During a reading of *Macbeth*, several students question Dorothy about the meaning of the line, "Macduff was from his mother's womb/Untimely ripp'd!" Half the children go home with the word "womb" on their lips, causing "a sudden commotion, a flying to and fro of messages, an electric thrill of horror through fifteen decent Nonconformist homes" (249).

The parents rally and hold a meeting with Mrs. Creevy. Orwell uses the scene to satirize middle-class prudery and anti-intellectualism, as one parent protests, "'We don't send our children to school to have ideas put into their heads.'" Dorothy argues that she was simply providing an explanation, but the parents' rage at this round about sex education from a virgin becomes a firestorm of sexual paranoia against "dirty films" and "dirty love-stories." The spokesperson for the parents insists that "'. . . we try to bring our children up decent and save them from knowing anything about the Facts of Life. If I had my way, no child—at any rate, no girl—would know anything about the Facts of Life until she was twenty-one'" (251-252).

In response to the protest, Mrs. Creevy restricts Dorothy's teaching methods to mindless drill work. Dorothy lives a nun's life of self-denial, hard work, filthy food, and loneliness. She masters, in Orwell's terms, the "dismal arts of the schoolteacher" (281).

Warburton, the lecher, writes Dorothy and comes to London to escort her home. In a reverse of *Burmese Days*, the novel ends with Warburton encouraging Dorothy to marry him in order to save herself from a sexless "death in life existence." He states his proposal in terms of a "bargain." "'Why should you spend your life delivering parish magazines and rubbing nasty old women's legs with Elliman's embrocation? You'd be happier married, even to a husband with a bald head and a clouded past'" (302). He asks Dorothy to consider what her future will entail— "'the same future that lies before any woman of our class with no husband and no money'":

> "After ten years . . . your father will die, and he will leave you with not a penny, only debts. You will be nearly forty, with no money, no profession, no chance of marrying; just a derelict parson's daughter like the ten thousand others in England. . . You'll have to get a job—the sort of job that parsons' daughters get. . . And all the time withering, drying up, growing more sour and more angular and more friendless." (302-305)

Though bald, middle-aged, and encumbered with three children he cheerfully calls "the bastards," Warburton offers her a secure, comfortable life. He attempts to seduce her with visions of pleasant surroundings, books, vacations, friends—a life that tempts Dorothy until she realizes this new life would require performing *all that*. So of course she says No, fully accepting Warburton's grim view of her future.

Although she no longer believes in God, she returns to her father's household and church duties, to a routine of rummage sales, sick calls, Sunday-school pageants, and thankless drudgery. Like Gordon Comstock, she comes full circle to accept the very life she had a chance to escape.

A Clergyman's Daughter is populated with female characters, nearly all of them Dickensian eccentrics—women marked by ugliness, petty meanness, and sour dispositions. Not one leads an apparently normal life, and not one appears to have a healthy attitude towards sex. Orwell seems preoccupied with chronicling unattractive women. In church Dorothy accepts the communion chalice after Miss Mayfill, whose "mouth was surprisingly large, loose, and wet. The under lip, pendulous with age, slobbered forward, exposing a strip of gum and a row of false teeth as yellow as the keys of an old piano" (14). Mrs. Semprill, the town gossip, is obsessed with tales of sodomy, illegitimate babies, orgies, and adulteries. Her "delicate red mouth" whispers perverse secrets into Dorothy's ear. Dorothy, and most of the townspeople, refuses to believe her tales of sexual perversion. Yet, Orwell notes Mrs. Semprill was "instrumental in breaking off of not less than half a dozen engagements and starting innumerable quarrels between husbands and wives" (54).

Dorothy's employer, Mrs. Creevy is described as a crabbed, ugly witch of a woman:

> Though she was not in the least dirty or untidy there was something discoloured about her whole appearance, as though she lived all her life in a bad light; and the expression of her mouth, sullen and ill-shaped

> with the lower lip turned down, recalled that of a toad. . . You could tell her at a glance for a person who knew exactly what she wanted, and would grasp it as ruthlessly as any machine; not a bully exactly . . . but a person who would make use of you and then throw you aside with no more compunction than if you had been a worn-out scrubbing brush.
> (216)

Though a school proprietor, Mrs. Creevy boasts of having never read a book through. Serving breakfast, she slices two eggs into strips, dividing them so that Dorothy receives only two-thirds of an egg. A wholly joyless creature, she is stingy and wages a war against a diffident male neighbor who happened to complain to the landlord that her chimney should be raised to prevent smoke from entering his windows:

> The very day the landlord's letter reached her, Mrs. Creevy called in the bricklayers and had the chimney lowered two feet. It cost her thirty shillings, but it was worth it. After that there had been the long guerrilla campaign of throwing things over the garden wall during the night, and Mrs. Creevy had finally won with a dustbinful of wet ashes thrown on to Mr. Boulger's bed of tulips. . . . Discovering by chance that the roots of Mr. Boulger's plum tree had grown under the wall into her own garden, she promptly injected a whole tin of weed-killer into them and killed the tree. This was remarkable as being the only occasion when Dorothy ever heard Mrs. Creevy laugh. (237)

Mrs. Creevy, whose garments bear the "impress of a frozen and awful chastity", employs desperately impoverished women teachers. Miss Strong, who preceded Dorothy, was an alcoholic. Miss Beaver, who had graduated to four pounds a week "after twenty years of slave-driving," lives in a cramped bedsitting room. Her free time is spent brewing tea, doing crossword puzzles, and looking at a photo album of her 1913 trip to Austria. "Her soul," Orwell states, "seemed to have withered until it was as forlorn as a dried-up cake of soap in a forgotten soap dish" (280).

In contrast to these female eccentrics, Dorothy seems, despite her frigidity, nearly normal. She is fully aware of her future:

> Dorothy perceived that by one of two well-beaten roads every third-rate schoolmistress must travel: Miss Strong's road, via whisky to the workhouse; or Miss Beaver's road, via strong tea to a decent death in the Home for Decayed Gentlewomen. (280)

Eager to escape dreary Mrs. Creevy, Dorothy seeks refuge, not in whisky or strong tea, but in George Gissing:

> She ate her Christmas dinner—a hard-boiled egg, two cheese sandwiches and a bottle of lemonade—in the woods near Burnham, against a great gnarled beech-tree, over a copy of George Gissing's *The Odd Women*. (277)

At first glance, Gissing's *The Odd Women* is an unlikely novel to win Orwell's praise as "one of the best novels in English." Orwell had little sensitivity to women or their social roles. As feminist critics have pointed out, Orwell examined political and economic issues in almost exclusively male terms. In *The Road to Wigan Pier* Orwell does present a moving portrait of a slum girl he sees from a train kneeling beside a clogged drainpipe—"the slum girl who is twenty-five and looks forty, thanks to miscarriages and drudgery." In her face, Orwell briefly saw "the most desolate, hopeless expression I have ever seen. . . She knew well enough what was happening to her—understood as well as I did how dreadful a destiny it was to be kneeling there in the bitter cold, on the slimy stones of a slum backyard, poking a stick up a foul drain-pipe" (*Road* 29).

But Orwell seemed less able to create moving portraits of women in his fiction. Gissing's *The Odd Women*, no doubt, fascinated him because of the novel's capacity to capture female characters more realistically than most Victorian literature of the time. The novel, though driven by standard plot devices and literary conventions, did focus on women's issues. It captured

Orwell's imagination largely because of the role money played in the characters lives:

> In *The Odd Women* there is not a single major character whose life is not ruined either by having too little money, or by getting it too late in life, or by the pressure of social conventions which are obviously absurd but which cannot be questioned. An elderly spinster crowns a useless life by taking to drink; a pretty young girl marries a man old enough to be her father; a struggling school-master puts off marrying his sweetheart until both of them are middle-aged and withered; a good-natured man is nagged to death by his wife; an exceptionally intelligent, spirited man misses his chance to make an adventurous marriage and relapses into futility; in each case the ultimate reason for the disaster lies in obeying the accepted social code, or in not having enough money to circumvent it. (*CEJL* IV 430)

The Odd Women tracks the fates of the six Madden sisters. As in Gissing's *Demos*, an inheritance or rather the lack of one plays a critical role in determining the fates of the protagonists. In the first chapter, entitled "The Fold and the Shepherd," set in 1872, Dr. Madden, a prominent physician, tells her eldest daughter Alice of his plan to insure his life for a thousand pounds. "'Let men grapple with the world,'" he tells her, asserting his desire that his daughters will never "'have to distress themselves about money matters'" (*Odd* 1). Madden maintained an intellectual household but provided no professional training to his children because the idea of his daughters "having to work for money was so utterly repulsive to him that he could never seriously dwell upon it" (*Odd* 3). At forty-nine, he anticipates that in ten or fifteen years his medical practice will generate sufficient wealth to safely provide for his girls. But, returning from a medical emergency, Madden is killed in a road accident, leaving his six daughters only eight hundred pounds.

Chapter Two, set some fifteen years later, reveals the fate of the Madden sisters. Three of the girls have died before reaching thirty. Gertrude died of consumption; Martha has drowned in a boating accident. Isabel, "worked into illness," suffered melancholia and was sent to a mental institution where she drowned herself at twenty-two. The survivors subsist on meager incomes derived from female occupations. Alice Madden teaches; Virginia serves as a lady's companion; Monica works for a draper. Both Alice and Virginia, past thirty and exhausted, despair of ever marrying, pinning their hopes on youthful Monica.

In describing the crabbed existences of Mrs. Creevy, Dorothy, and Miss Beaver, Orwell clearly was inspired by Gissing's depiction of the Maddens. Though not yet thirty-five, the older sisters live like elderly spinsters. Dining on mashed potatoes and milk, they go to bed by nine-thirty to save lamp oil. Monica, just twenty and attractive, despairs over her sisters' plight:

> Their loneliness was for life, poor things. Already they were old; and they would grow older, sadder, perpetually struggling to supplement that dividend from the precious capital—and merely that they might keep alive. Oh!—her heart ached at the misery of such a prospect. How much better if the poor girls had never been born. (*Odd* 31)

But unlike Orwell's novel, *The Odd Women* presents a pair of progressive women whom Gissing develops as full characters, not caricatures. Mary Barfoot and her protégé Rhoda Nunn operate a school that trains women for non-traditional employment. As Orwell noted, Gissing was dubious about politics and social activism. But Gissing clearly approves of Barfoot's educational project:

> She did not seek to become known as the leader of a "movement," yet her quiet work was probably more effectual than the public career of women who propagandize for female emancipation. Her aim was to draw from the overstocked profession of teaching as many capable young women as she could lay hands on, and to fit them for certain of the pursuits nowadays thrown open to their sex. She held the conviction that whatever man could do, woman could do equally well—those tasks

only excepted which demand great physical strength. (*Odd* 54)

Gissing is far more sympathetic to Barfoot's feminism than the Socialism embraced by Richard Mutimer in *Demos*. This sympathy stems in part from Barfoot's disdain for the poor, which matches Gissing's own prejudices. "'I choose my sphere,'" she explains, announcing, "'Let those work for the lower classes (I must call them lower, for they are, in every sense), let those work for them who have a call to do so. I have none. I must keep to my own class'" (*Odd* 53). Moreover, her radicalism is based on facts rather than ideology. She is not wholly against marriage, but argues that women must have alternatives:

> ". . . do you know that there are half a million more women than men in this happy country of ours?
> . . . . So many *odd* women—no making a pair with them. The pessimists call them useless, lost, futile lives. I, naturally—being one of them myself—take another view. I look upon them as a great reserve.
> (*Odd* 37)

Unlike Mutimer's ego-driven Socialist harangues in *Demos*, the statements Gissing creates for Mary Barfoot form sensible and quite advanced—for the 1890s—editorials on behalf of women. In all his essays, Orwell never devoted as much sustained attention to the social position of women Gissing offers in a few pages of *The Odd Women*. Mary Barfoot's speech about women in part reflects Gissing's own observations of "paltry women":

> "Womanly and womanish are two very different words; but the latter, as the world uses it, has become practically synonymous with the former. A womanly occupation means, practically, an occupation that a man disdains. And here is the root of the matter.
> . . . . I am a troublesome, aggressive, revolutionary person. I want to do away with that common confusion of the words womanly and womanish, and I see very clearly that this can only be effected by an armed movement, an invasion by women of the spheres which men

have always forbidden us to enter.... Were we living in an ideal world, I think women would not go to sit all day in offices. But the fact is that we live in a world as far from ideal as can be conceived. We live in a time of warfare, of revolt. If woman is no longer to be womanish, but a human being of powers and responsibilities, she must become militant, defiant. She must push her claims to the extremity...

.... Let a woman be gentle, but at the same time let her be strong; let her be pure of heart, but none the less wise and instructed.... The mass of women have always been paltry creatures, and their paltriness has proved a curse to men. So, if you like to put it in this way, we are working for the advantage of men as well as for our own."

(*Odd* 135-137)

Barfoot's feminist invasion would create the ideal Gissing woman, feminine yet intelligent, realistic but not crass. Gissing, whose characters suffered from female paltriness, approves of Barfoot's new woman—a strong, soft female less driven to seek security through marriage.

Barfoot's brother, Everard, shares her values and falls in love with her ardent lieutenant, Rhoda Nunn. "Let beauty perish if it cannot ally itself with mind; be a woman what else she may, let her have brains and the power of using them!," he argues (*Odd* 176). This desire for an intelligent spouse reflects what Gissing terms Everard's "maturity of his manhood." However, in typical Gissing fashion, Everard also admits, "For casual amour the odalisque could still prevail with him" (*Odd* 176). Intellect, for Everard, was strictly a wifely requirement.

But in a society layered in social convention, marriage in *The Odd Women* remains a dubious venture. Gissing uses the term "marriage war" to describe Monica Madden's thoughts regarding a suitor old enough to be her father. Slaving eighty hours a week behind a draper's counter, Monica sees marriage as a tempting escape. She marries Edmund Widdowson, a stiff middle-aged man who preaches strict obedience to traditional values, "'You shall read Ruskin,'" he tells his young bride, "'every word he says about women is good and precious.... I sincerely believe that an educated woman had better become a domestic servant than try to imitate the life of a man'" (*Odd* 153).

Within months both are miserable. Monica feels stifled. She comes to loathe the sight of her husband, whose "face was repulsive to her" (*Odd* 225). She seeks escape through a relationship with a younger man, hoping to find "swift, virile passion, eagerness even to anticipate her desire of flight, a strength, a courage to which she could abandon herself, body and soul" (*Odd* 231). Suspecting his wife, Widdowson "burns" with jealousy, pounding the pavement with "a constable's regularity" (252). Discovering she is pregnant, Monica resolves not to return home to avoid the suspicion of having committed adultery. Monica falls ill and, like three other Madden sisters, dies prematurely, leaving behind a newborn daughter. Rhoda Nunn vows to care for the infant and "make a brave woman of her" (336).

But if Gissing depicts conventional Victorian marriage as a bleak institution, he shows that even those who attempt to break the mold are casualties of the marriage war.

Everard Barfoot seeks Rhoda as his ideal woman, telling her, "you have had enough of books. It's time to live" (261). Wanting her to abandon her ideals to become his wife, Barfoot tests her with an offer of marriage "without forms of mutual bondage." Driven to see the zealous feminist inspired with "unreflecting passion," he makes his proposal, stating, "If we cannot trust each other without legal bonds, any union between us would be unjustified" (264). Their illegal relationship, he assures her, would be kept from everyone but their closest friends.

Sexually aroused and stirred by the idea of a bold break from convention, Rhoda is excited, "she decided that the sensational step was preferable to a commonplace renunciation of all she had so vehemently preached" (*Odd* 264). Pressed by Everard for an answer, she demands more time. Embracing her, he slips a wedding band on her hand. Recoiling from the "perilous symbol," Rhoda rejects his offer, stating "Custom is too strong for us. We should only play at defying it" (266). She encourages Everard to obtain a marriage license.

But "neither was content." Reflecting on their meeting, Barfoot realizes that "as usual the woman had her way"(268). Rhoda was not the "glorious rebel" he imagined her to be. Like other women she shrank from any sexual relationship not cemented in social convention and legal sanction. Although she had triumphed, Rhoda, too, is dissatisfied, doubting Everard's sympathy with the women's movement. Though she is "no longer one of the 'odd women'. . . none the less her sense of mission remained" (270). The prospect of domestic life and possible motherhood leads to further doubts.

Like John Flory and Elizabeth in *Burmese Days*, Barfoot and Nunn are victims of a quirk of fate. Rhoda receives a letter from Mary Barfoot stating that a detective hired by Widdowson followed Monica to Everard's flat. The letter produces accusations and counter accusations between Everard and Rhoda. Angered by Barfoot's attitude and her own sexual desires, Rhoda determines to reject him, persuading "herself not only that the thought of Everard Barfoot was hateful to her soul, but that sexual love had become, and would ever be, to her an impure idea, a vice of blood" (281).

But, as Gissing asserts, the "vice of blood" is not easily abjured. She suffers in "mute frenzy," the "passions of her flesh tormenting her until she thought of death as a refuge" (283). In the chapter titled "Retreat with Honor," Rhoda and Everard confront each other a final time, their roles reversed. Now Barfoot offers legal marriage, an institution Rhoda now rejects. They part; two weeks later Barfoot announces his engagement to another woman.

Although Orwell greatly admired *The Odd Women*, his own novel of an "odd woman" is thinly superficial. Despite living a half-century after Gissing's protagonists, Dorothy Hare seems more bound to convention than her Victorian sisters. She lacks the depth of emotion of Rhoda Nunn and the insight of Mary Barfoot. Orwell's view of the "marriage war" is limited to Dorothy's simplistic frigidity. Unlike Gissing's women, Dorothy feels no conflict; she simply rejects marriage on one principle—marriage implies intercourse. Faced with the dreaded "all that," Dorothy has to "say No" to the aging lecher as she did to the young curate.

Significantly, it is a male character who echoes Mary Barfoot's observations on the hundreds of thousands of "odd women." Removing his hat to expose his bald head, Warburton presents himself in the humblest light and offers Dorothy a bargain, "'You need a home and a livelihood; I need a wife to keep me in order'" (*Clergyman's* 301-302). He sketches her future if she fails to marry as "that slavish, worrying life" of caring for her aging and disagreeable father. "'Every year,'" he warns her, "'your life will be a little bleaker, a little fuller of those deadly little jobs that are shoved off on to lonely women. And remember that you won't always be twenty-eight. All the while you will be fading, withering, until one morning you will look in the glass and realise that you aren't a girl any longer, only a skinny old maid'" (303). Though selfish, the aging lecher objectively understands the plight of women without a career or a marriage, the women Rhoda Nunn calls a "ragged regiment."

Instead of arguing with Warburton's dismal view of her future, Dorothy accepts and embraces it as her only possible life. Although she has lost her religious faith, she returns to serve her father, dedicating herself to Sunday-school pageants and jumble sales. She accepts being an odd woman as one accepts mortality, enlisting in the ragged regiment for life.

SEVEN
DOOMED UTOPIAS: *ANIMAL FARM* AND *DEMOS*

> "It's him as is rich now, an' where's the difference 'tween him and them as he called names?"
>
> Gissing, *Demos*

> The creatures outside looked from pig to man, and from man to pig, and from pig to man again; but already it was impossible to say which was which.
>
> Orwell, *Animal Farm*

George Gissing subtitled his 1886 novel, "A Story of English Socialism." A reactionary tragedy, *Demos* presents an *Animal Farm* drama of a revolution corrupted through greed and power lust. As in Orwell's parable, the seeds of corruption are inherent at the beginning. But whereas Orwell sought to analyze the faults of a system, Gissing's antipathy was directed against a class.

Gissing had little love of capitalism. As stated by David Grylls, Gissing grew up viewing business as a narrow-minded and philistine enterprise. Although Gissing's father was a chemist and small business owner, he consciously separated his children from those of other tradespeople. Gissing's brother William criticized the "mean money-making spirit which is the bane of the world—no music, no poetry, no love in it, only one everlasting stubborn fight" (qtd. Grylls 56-57). Gissing's own view of capitalism is best expressed in his depiction of the Morgan family in *In The Year of the Jubilee*.

As London suburbanites, the Morgans are both victims and victimizers. As consumers they are duped by advertising into buying a cheaply built house. As homeowners they are forced to exploit others to maintain their lifestyle. Their new home stands on a plot which once belonged to a wooded estate. To make way for progress, "Great elms, the pride of generations passed away, fell before the speculative axe" (*Jubilee* 196). Because of developer's greed, the "very earth had lost its wholesome odour; trampled into mire, fouled with builders' refuse and the noisome drift from adjacent streets, it sent forth, under the sooty rain, a smell of corruption. . ." (196-197). As soon as the Morgans move into their new house advertised to be "'handsomely decorated'" it begins to deteriorate—"Not a door that would close as a door should; not a window that would open in the way expected of it; not a fireplace but discharged its smoke into the room. . . . From cellar floor to chimney-pot, no square inch of honest or trustworthy workmanship" (197).

To support himself in this crumbling dream house, Mr. Morgan enters a collection agency, justifying his actions by his needs:

> A man of mild temper and humane instincts, he spent his day in hunting people who would not or could pay the money they owed. . . The occupation revolted him, but at present he saw no other way of supporting the genteel appearances which—he knew not why—were indispensable to his life. He subsisted like a bird of prey; he was ever on the look out for carrion which the law permitted him to seize. From the point of view forced upon him, society became a mere system of legalized rapine. "You are in debt; hold the bond. Behold, too, my authority for squeezing out of you the uttermost farthing. You must beg or starve? I deplore it, but I, for my part, have a genteel family to maintain on what I rend from your grip." (*Jubilee* 198)

But Gissing, despite a youthful flirtation with Positivism, did not view social restructuring as a necessary instrument to social progress. Gissing would have probably shared Orwell's perception that, "We are living in a world in which nobody is free, in which hardly anybody is secure, in which it is almost impossible to be honest and remain alive" (*Road* 144). Gissing would also agree with Orwell's observation that "Socialism, in the form which it is now presented to us, has about it something inherently distasteful" (*Road* 145). Most distasteful for Gissing would be Orwell's view that "Socialism, *in the form in which it is now presented*, appeals chiefly to unsatisfactory or even inhuman types" (*Road* 153). Gissing would not have bothered with Orwell's italicized qualification. For him, the problem Socialism presented was that it countered the abuses of capitalism by empowering "inhuman types."

Gissing, the classicist, frames his "Story of English Socialism" in terms of a Greek drama of blatant *hubris*. *Demos* is less a condemnation of Socialism than a moral argument that people of the lower classes should know their place and remain there. It is not only that the political system is wrong in itself; it is denounced because its exponent is an articulate, self-educated —and therefore dangerous—member of the working class. Especially repugnant to Gissing is the notion of a working class male embracing an upper class lady. As in *New Grub Street*, the plot of *Demos* turns on the struggle of two romantic rivals. The protagonist marries the heroine, but once widowed, she quickly falls for her husband's counterpart.

The protagonist of *Demos* is Richard Mutimer, a politically active mechanical engineer. "Richard represented . . . the best qualities his class can show," Gissing states of his main character. His physique is described as "admirable." But Mutimer, though the best of his class, is clearly marked by subtle inferiorities; his eyes, for example, are "keen and direct; but they had small variety of expression; you could not imagine them softening to tenderness, or even to thoughtful dreaming" (*Demos* 33). Mutimer is clearly a product of the working class and therefore in Gissing's eyes, hopelessly limited because he has a distorted notion of his own talents, "a distinct consciousness of his points of superiority to the men among whom he lived" (33).

Most disturbing in Gissing's eyes is Mutimer's zealous championing of Socialism and his increasing appetite for power:

> One saw from his way of speaking, that he believed himself about to become a popular hero; already in imagination he stood forth on platforms before vast assemblies, and heard his own voice denouncing capitalism with force which nothing could resist. The first taste of applause had given extraordinary impulse to his convictions, and the personal ambition with which they were interwoven. (36)

The major flaw in Mutimer's character is his education. For Gissing, Mutimer represents the result of a debased culture and the universality of "free thought." Richard's library of self-selected books reveals his intellectual limitations, "to survey them was to understand the man" (42). Mutimer's bookcase is filled with "extreme" texts, "books which a bright youth of fair opportunities reads as a matter of course, rejoices in for a year or two, then throws aside forever" were for Mutimer "treasured to be the guides of a lifetime" (42). Among his books are sensational pamphlets extolling vegetarianism (one of Orwell's pet peeves) and the notion "that if every man and woman performed their quota of the world's labour it would be necessary to work for one hour and thirty-seven minutes daily" (42). These publications drive Gissing to despair:

> Alas, alas! On this food had Richard Mutimer pastured his soul since he grew to manhood, on this and this only. English literature was to him a sealed volume; poetry he scarcely knew by name; of history he was worse than ignorant, having looked at this period and that through distorting media, and congratulating himself on his clear vision because he saw men as trees walking. (42)

Gissing's private nightmare—that of the ardent unlettered zealot achieving power—is played out in the novel, though not through political revolution but a curiously Victorian chain of events involving a rich relative and a quirky will.

Ironmaster Mutimer attained wealth and status in the town of Wanley and purchased a grand manor house from the Eldons, an aristocratic family ruined by financial speculation. Mutimer, a man who knew his place, did not dislodge the impoverished Eldons for "they were the aristocracy of the neighborhood, and to have them ousted by a name which no one knew, a name connected only with blast-furnaces, would have made a distinct fall in the tone of Wanley society" (*Demos* 2).

Hubert Eldon, the surviving aristocratic son, returns to Wanley days after the ironmaster's death. Wounded in a duel on the Continent, Hubert is depicted as willful, spoiled, and immature. Gossip of his dissolute life reached England and Eldon repeatedly failed to respond to his mother's correspondence. To kind-hearted Mutimer, Eldon's refusal to answer his mother's entreaties was evidence of a severe character flaw. Sensing that Hubert Eldon is irresponsible, the ironmaster destroys his will. Instead of returning to the Eldon's, the estate is left to Mutimer's London relatives, working class people Hubert decries as being the "'roughest of the rough'" (15).

Richard Mutimer, lacking his benefactor's sense of place, delights in his inheritance and the power it grants him. "'Just because I've been born and bred a mechanic,'" he tells his mother, "'does that say I've got no common sense or self-respect?'" (46). Empowered with cash, Mutimer envisions himself as being a leader, "the gloried representative of his class . . . . crowds should throng to hear him; his gospel would be trumpeted over the land" (49).

For Mutimer, the iron works becomes a kind of Animal Farm, a capitalist industrial enterprise to be reworked on Socialist ideals to benefit the workers instead of enriching the factory owner:

> "I would begin by building furnaces, and in time add engineering works on a large scale. I would build houses for the men, and in fact make that valley an industrial settlement conducted on Socialist principles. Practically I can devote the whole of my income; my personal expenses will not be worth taking into account."(56)

But like the pigs in *Animal Farm*, Mutimer is immediately corrupted by power. After his first brief inspection tour, Mutimer notices a defect in the manor house. "'It's unfortunate,'" he notes, "'that the railway misses it by about three miles, but Rodman tells me we can easily run a private line to the Agworth station'"(58).

Yet Mutimer makes a solemn pledge, "'. . . if I live another fifty years I shall still be of the people and with the people, that no man shall ever have it in his power to say that Richard Mutimer misused his chances and was only a new burden to them whose load he might have lightened!'" (66).

For Gissing, Mutimer's *hubris* and threat to social order is demonstrated not only by his drive for power, but his ruthless attitude toward Nature. Like Orwell, Gissing was suspicious of development, of "progress" whether advanced by capitalist developers or Socialist reformers. Gissing would have echoed Orwell's concern for Socialism's fascination with technology, ". . . the unfortunate thing is that Socialism . . . is bound up with the idea of mechanical progress, not merely as a necessary development but as an end in itself, almost as a kind of religion"(*Road* 158).

Priest of the smokestack, Mutimer envisions massive industrial expansion. Speaking with the soon to be evicted Hubert Eldon, Mutimer describes his scheme to build factories on a grassy plain. "'In a year or two you won't know the place,'" he informs the dispossessed aristocrat (71). When Eldon states his preference for the existing landscape, Mutimer snorts with reformist zeal, "'The Wanley Iron Works will soon mean bread to several hundred families; how many would the grass support?'" (71).

Mutimer's position gives him power to indulge personal desires. Like the pigs in *Animal Farm*, he becomes increasingly corrupted, increasingly resembling the aristocrats he claims to despise. His sudden caprices drive him to possess a riding horse. Like Orwell's pigs, who confiscate windfall apples and grow barley to brew beer, Mutimer develops a taste for "sundry delicacies" he never tasted and could not pronounce, "so there appeared upon his breakfast table a *pate de foie gras*" (134). So, too, he comes to desire Adela Waltham, daughter of Wanley's most respected family. Mutimer throws over his working class girl friend in London for this woman of refinement. His cruel abandonment stems from a loss of moral character, because the "voice of his conscience lost potency, though it troubled him more than ever, even as a beggar will sometimes become rudely clamorous when he sees that there is no real hope of extracting an alms" (135). In Gissing's view, Mutimer's faults stem from the innate flaws of working class mentality:

> The fatal defect in working people is absence of imagination, the power which may be solely a gift of nature and irrespective of circumstances, but which in most of us owes so much to intellectual training. Half the brutal cruelties perpetrated by uneducated men and women are directly traceable to lack of the imaginative spirit, which comes to mean lack of kindly sympathy. (136)

As a result, Mutimer cannot comprehend the suffering he inflicts on his abandoned lover or those who get in the way of his aims. In addition to his intolerance, is his basic vulgarity, and for Gissing, "the vulgarity of a man who tries hard not to be vulgar is always particularly distressing" (183).

Having won Adela, Mutimer lectures her about his goals and principles. In the process, he exposes his growing hypocrisy. He refuses the title "employer", modestly proclaiming, "'I regulate the work, just because somebody must'" (186). Though announcing himself to be the modest "regulator," Mutimer presents himself as a Messiah, telling Adela, "'There's my religion, down there in New Wanley. I'm saving men and women and children from hunger and cold and the lives of brute beasts. I teach them to live honestly and soberly'"(187). Like Napoleon, Orwell's dictatorial pig, Mutimer espouses abstinence while drinking himself, "'There's no public-house in New Wanley,'" he states, "'and there won't be.' (It just flashed across Adela's mind that Mutimer drank wine himself)" (187).

When Mutimer's sister Alice arrives from London, the modest "regulator's" transformation into Napoleon is complete. Arriving at the station to meet her, he is troubled that a Mutimer has ridden in a second class railway carriage:

> ". . . it ought to have been first. In London things don't matter, but here I'm known, you see. . ."
> "Yes, you ought to have come first-class. A princess riding second'll never do . . ."
> ". . . And is this your own horse and trap, Dick?"
> "Of course it is."
> "Who was that man? He touched his hat to you."
> Mutimer glanced back carelessly.
> "I'm sure I don't know. Most people touch their hats to me about here."
>
> (193-194)

Once in the manor house, Mutimer directs his sister in dealing with servants. Now moneyed, Mutimer adopts the vices of the rich. He buys off his London girl friend, cavalierly dismissing her like a nobleman ridding himself of a pregnant domestic. Mutimer's mother, a working class woman exuding humility, offers a Greek chorus warning of her son's pride and ambition:

"Money! There you've hit the word; it's money as 'as ruined him, an as'll be the ruin of us all. . . Is all his feelings got as hard as money?. . . .
It's my belief as money's the curse o' this world. . . It's him as is rich now, an' where's the difference 'tween him and them as he called names?" (207)

Many of the workers come to share this view, denouncing Mutimer for "his shameless hypocrisy, his greed, his infernal arrogance" (239).

Mutimer is angered by growing resistance to his plans, beginning to see criticism as "impertinence." "What was the use of wealth," he contemplated, "if it did not exempt one from the petty laws binding on miserable hand-to-mouth toilers! . . . Men with large aims cannot afford to be scrupulous in small details. Was not New Wanley a sufficient balance against a piece of injustice. . .?"(244). In one instance Mutimer dismisses a worker allegedly for drinking, but the employee's real infraction was expressing disloyalty. "'He was impudent to me,'" he informs Adela, "'and I cannot allow that. He'll have to go'" (256). When Adela attempts to intercede on the worker's behalf, Mutimer refuses to reconsider his case because he does not wish to risk a loss of "authority." Daily Mutimer becomes more arrogant, "more ambitious and more punctilious in his intercourse with all whom . . . he deemed inferiors. . .(276-277).

Megalomania leads Mutimer to consider abandoning the New Wanley project when costs rise, threatening his personal wealth:

> Opposition, from whomsoever it came, aggravated him. He was more than ever troubled about the prospects of New Wanley; there even loomed before his mind a possible abandonment of the undertaking. He had never contemplated the sacrifice of his fortune, and though anything of that kind was still very far off, it was daily more difficult for him to face with equanimity even moderate losses. Money had fostered ambition, and ambition full grown had more need than ever of its nurse. New Wanley was no longer an end in itself, but a stepping-stone. (278)

With his aggravation, Mutimer shows an increasing tendency to act cruelly and unfairly. This "crude tyranny" is heightened in Gissing's view because of his pronounced "lack of native or acquired refinement" (300).

The turning point in the novel occurs when Adela accidentally discovers old Mutimer's will in a private church pew. The document undoes what Gissing clearly views as an error, restoring Hubert Eldon as the rightful heir and bequeathing to Richard Mutimer a modest annuity of one hundred and seven pounds a year. The language of the will stings Mutimer with a patronizing judgment Gissing shared about his protagonist:

> "It is not my wish"—these words followed the directions—"to put the said Richard Mutimer above the need of supporting himself by honest work, but only to aid him to make use of the abilities which I understand he possesses, and to become a credit to the class to which he belongs." (311)

Mutimer instantly dismisses the document as a forgery. He rejects Adela's observation that the paper had been covered by dust and could not be a recent invention. "'Of course. They wouldn't bungle over an important thing like this,'" he asserts (314). Adela is disturbed by her husband's suspicions because any conspiracy would by definition implicate the discoverer of a forged document. She suggests that an attorney examine the will for authenticity. "'If this is forged,'" Mutimer reasons, "'the lawyer has of course given his help'" (315). Hoping to secure her silence on the matter, Mutimer argues that he rather than Eldon is the rightful heir. Eldon would "'spend it on himself, like other rich men. It isn't every day that a man of my principles gets the means of putting them in practice . . . The good of thousands, of hundred of thousands, is at stake,'" he tells his wife (318). Adela insists that good works cannot be based on deception, and reluctantly, Mutimer agrees to meet with an attorney who verifies the will's authenticity.

Now in possession of the iron works, Hubert Eldon informs Adela of his plans, "'I shall sweep away every trace of the mines and the works and the houses, and do my utmost to restore the valley to its former state'" (338). To Eldon, the Socialist development represents "desolation and defilement" of "one of the loveliest spots to be found in England" (338). In announcing his plans to restore the landscape, Eldon asserts a pro-nature, anti-machine view similar to Orwell's observations in *The Road to Wigan Pier*. "'It may be inevitable that the green and beautiful spots of the world shall give place to furnaces and mechanics' dwellings. For my own part, in this little corner, at all events, the ruin shall be delayed . . . . Of New Wanley not one brick shall remain on another'" (338). Asked if he values the grass over people, Eldon responds with the statement, "'I had rather say that I see no value in human lives in a world from which grass and trees have vanished'"(339).

Ever the egoist, Mutimer relishes his loss of fortune, determining "to make the most of abdication" (341). Sensing his decline would make him a martyr to the cause, Mutimer seeks power through a political movement. He announces plans to write a book about his attempt. His goal is to make his name known in London's East End. "'What we want is personal influence,'" he argues, justifying his cult of personality with the observation, "'It's no use asking them to get excited about a *movement*; they must have a *man* . . . He talked for three hours, at times as if he were already on the platform before a crowd of East Enders who were shouting 'Mutimer forever!'"(403). Mutimer's drive for power leads him into a political re-evaluation. Just as the pigs in *Animal Farm* justify doing business with humans and trading in money, so Mutimer devises a capitalistic investment scheme. He plans to collect three pence a week from workers whom he is convinced would only spend the money on drink and instead "put it out to interest." Inflated with the magic concept of "interest" and the delightfully better "compound interest," Mutimer envisions the power he will gain. "'Don't you see,'" he tells Adela, "'that it'll give me a hold over them?'" (413). Mutimer abandons Socialism for the more lucrative concept of Democratic Capitalism. Like Orwell's pigs who are stung with counterfeit notes, Mutimer, blinded by greed, invests in a politically appealing venture called the Irish Dairy Company promising a thirty-percent return. Mutimer's ego soars to its greatest heights when he remarks to his wife, "'I say, Adela, how would it sound —"Richard Mutimer, First President of the English Republic?"'" (429).

Mutimer and his followers are swindled. Three thousand penny investors become a "tempest of savage faces" and form a blood-thirsty mob, "Demos was having its way; civilisation was blotted out, and club law proclaimed" (454). Fleeing for his life, Mutimer takes shelter in his old girl friend's house. Attempting to speak to the crowd from a window, Mutimer is struck by a rock and killed.

Gissing ends his "Story of English Socialism" by literally turning back the clock, so that "In all the valley no trace is left of what was called New Wanley" (462). Gissing delights that the valley has been cleansed "as if the foot of Demos had never come that way" (461). What is important in this celebration of nature is Gissing's contempt not only for Socialism but for industrial enterprise:

> Incredible that the fume of furnaces ever desecrated that fleece-sown sky of tenderest blue, that hammers clanged and engines roared where now the thrush utters his song so joyously. Hubert Eldon has been as good as his word. . . . Once more we can climb to the top Stanbury Hill and enjoy the sense of remoteness and security. . . . (461-462).

Gissing's view of "progress" is limited to the cultivation of the sensible intellect of the spiritually aristocratic. Taking refuge with a friend, Mutimer's widow realizes that progress does not require "political" or even "social" action:

> ... there is a work in the cause of humanity other than that which goes on so clamorously in lecture-halls and at street corners, other than that which is silently performed by faithful hearts and hands in dens of misery and amid the horrors of the lazar-house; the work of those whose soul is taken captive of loveliness, who pursue the spiritual ideal apart from the world's tumult, and, ever ready to minister in gentle offices, know that they serve best when nearest home. (470)

On the final page of *Demos* Adela achieves her "womanhood" by falling in love with Hubert Eldon, the destroyer of her husband's Socialist utopia.

Although Orwell clearly had little sympathy for Gissing's political beliefs, he placed *Demos* along with *New Grub Street* and *The Odd Women* as novels which led him to maintain "that England has produced very few better novelists" (*CEJL* IV 433). Despite its reactionary sermonizing, *Demos* expresses one of Orwell's deepest concerns about Socialism, its reliance on industrialism and the implied exploitation of nature. Both Orwell and Gissing denounced the rush to industrialized development and the loss of nature, whether motivated for profit or progress. Though Orwell would hardly endorse Hubert Eldon, he did share his sense that there is something sacred, valuable about "the green and beautiful spots of the world."

EIGHT
LEAVES OF GRASS

> ". . . I have a sort of belly-to-earth attitude and always feel uneasy when I get away from the ordinary world where grass is green, stones hard, etc."
>
> Orwell, Letter to Henry Miller

> "For more than six years I trod the pavement, never stepping once upon mother earth—for the parks are but pavement disguised with a growth of grass."
>
> Gissing, *The Private Papers of Henry Ryecroft*

Gissing ended *Demos* with an environmentalist's wish fulfillment vision of bucolic Erewhon erasing all traces of a smoke belching ironworks. Despite the novel's reactionary politics, this scene must have appealed to Orwell who valued nature:

Isn't there, therefore, something sentimental and obscurantist in preferring bird-song to swing music and in wanting to leave a few patches of wildness here and there instead of covering the whole surface of the earth with a network of *Autobahnen* flooded with artificial sunlight?" (*CEJL* IV 81).

Hubert Eldon's love of beautiful green places, Orwell asserted, should not be viewed as sentimental or politically reactionary. Like Gissing, Orwell sensed that the rush toward technological progress, driven by capitalism or Five Year Plans, was steadily dehumanizing civilization:

> Man needs warmth, society, leisure, comfort and security: he also needs solitude, creative work and the sense of wonder. If he recognized this he could use the products of science and industrialism eclectically, applying always the same test: does this make me more human or less human. . . . For man only stays human by preserving large patches of simplicity in his life, while the tendency of many modern inventions... is to weaken his consciousness, dull his curiosity, and, in general, drive him nearer to the animals . (*CEJL* IV 81)

Orwell shared Gissing's mistrust of technology, even innocuous inventions designed solely for comfort. Both questioned, for example, the desirability of central heating. For Gissing, there was nothing more comforting than the English hearth:

> A fire is a delightful thing, a companion and an inspiration. If my room were kept warm by some wretched modern contrivance of water-pipes or heated air, would it be the same to me as that beautiful core of glowing fuel, which, if I sit and gaze into it, becomes a world of wonders? Let science warm the heaven-forsaken inhabitants of flats and hotels as effectually and economically as it may; if the choice were forced upon me, I had rather sit like an Italian, wrapped in my mantel, softly stirring with a key the silver-grey surface of the brasier's charcoal . . . . Because, in the course of nature, it will be some day a thing of the past (like most other things that are worth living for), is that a reason why it should not be enjoyed as long as possible? Human beings may ere long take their nourishment in the form of pills; the prevision of that happy economy causes me no reproach when I sit down to a joint of meat. (*Ryecroft* 139-140)

Orwell also focused on the English hearthside as something of intrinsic value, a source of inspiration threatened by mechanical progress:

> I have often been struck by the peculiar easy completeness, the perfect symmetry as it were, of a working-class interior at its best. Especially on winter evenings after tea, when the fire glows in the open range and dances mirrored in the steel fender, when Father, in shirt-sleeves, sits in the rocking chair at one side of the fire reading the racing finals, and Mother sits on the other with her sewing, and the children are happy with a pennorth of mint humbugs, and the dog lolls roasting himself on the rag mat....
> ....Skip forward two hundred years into the Utopian future, and the scene is totally different. Hardly one of the things I have imagined will still be there. In that age when there is no manual labor and everyone is "educated," it is hardly likely that Father will still be a rough man with enlarged hands... And there won't be a coal fire in the grate, only some kind of invisible heater. The furniture will be made of rubber, glass and steel.... Dogs, too, will have been suppressed on grounds of hygiene. And there won't be so many children, either, if the birth-controllers have their way. (*Road* 104-105)

As far as taking nourishment in the form of pills, Orwell bitterly complained about the artificiality of "factory-made, foil-wrapped cheeses," the "hideous rows of tins," and "the filthy chemical by-product that people will pour down their throats under the name of beer" (*Road* 170). Orwell's concern about the nature of English food follows Gissing's observation that the "deterioration of English butter is one of the worst signs of the moral state of our people" (*Ryecroft* 152).

Gissing and Orwell outlined similar manifestos on nature in characteristically dissimilar books. Gissing's observations were expressed in one of his last books, a novel written in the form of a retired writer's journal, *The Private Papers of Henry Ryecroft*. The book's preface purports to be an editor's commentary on his discovery of and decision to publish the contents of deceased Ryecroft's last writings. Posing as the editor, Gissing explains his rationale of dividing the book into four chapters named after the seasons because of Ryecroft's frequent references to nature.

Henry Ryecroft, like Gissing, is a New Grub Street writer. A "man of independent and rather scornful outlook," he toiled for years at hackwork, writing reviews, translations, and articles. Ryecroft, like Edmund Reardon, labored at literature like a manual worker, churning out pages to wrench out a marginal living in the literary marketplace.

At fifty, Ryecroft inherited an annuity allowing him to spend the last three years of his life in comfort and contemplation in the English countryside. Having resided in cosmopolitan London for decades, the man of letters dwelled on nature, ensuring that the "last thought of my brain as I lie dying will be that of sunshine upon an English meadow" (*Ryecroft* 57).

Although intended as a investigative journalist's account of housing and employment conditions in the north of England in the 1930s, Orwell's *The Road to Wigan Pier* serves in part as Orwell's treatise on nature and technology. Like Gissing's novel, Orwell's book asserts that nature, which is necessary for humans to retain their humanity, is consistently undermined by progress. Both Gissing and Orwell express the view that industrial and scientific development is inevitable and will have unwholesome side effects which are largely overlooked in the rush to improve society. Both distrust visions of Utopias that envision a future shaped by science and invention.

Nature, Gissing and Orwell argue, is more than a source of beauty or a tonic, it is a soul-restoring, almost spiritual force countering the glumness, grubbiness, and soul-crushing conformity of modern society symbolized in their novels by London. The joy of nature inspired Ryecroft when burdened by his need to grind out mediocre literary material to support himself:

> How I dreaded the white page I had to foul with ink! Above all, on days such as this, when the blue eyes of Spring laughed from between rosy clouds, when the sunlight shimmered upon my table and made me

long, long all but to madness, for the scent of the flowering earth, for the green of hillside larches, for the singing of the skylark above the downs. (*Ryecroft* 11)

Emerging by train from the soot of one northern factory town on his way to another, Orwell delighted that "even in the filthy heart of civilisation you find fields where the grass is green instead of grey; perhaps if you looked for them you might even find streams with live fish in them instead of salmon tins" (*Wigan* 30). Looking out the window, he was captivated by appearance of spring:

> Although the snow was hardly broken the sun was shining brightly. . . . According to the almanac this was spring, and a few of the birds seemed to believe it. For the first time in my life, in a bare patch beside the line, I saw rooks treading. . . . I had hardly been in the train half an hour, but it seemed a very long way from the Brookers' back-kitchen to the empty slopes of snow, the bright sunshine and the big gleaming birds. (*Wigan* 30)

The opening chapter of Henry Ryecroft's journal includes a scene in which the author recalls leaving his "grim lodgings" in London for an impromptu trip to the Devon countryside. Away from the chartered streets, amid the beauties of nature, Ryecroft undergoes a life-altering metamorphosis:

> The light, the air, had for me something of the supernatural—affected me, indeed, only less than at a later time did the atmosphere of Italy. It was glorious spring weather; a few white clouds floated amid the blue, and the earth had an intoxicating fragrance. Then first did I know myself for a sunworshipper. . . . I went bare-headed, that the golden beams might shed me their unstinted blessing. . .
>
> I had stepped into a new life. Between the man I had been and that which I now became there was a very notable difference. In a single day I had matured astonishingly; which means, no doubt, that I suddenly entered into conscious enjoyment of powers and sensibilities which had been developing unknown to me. To instance only one point: till then I had cared very little about plants and flowers, but now I found myself

> eagerly interested in every blossom, in every growth of the wayside. . . . To me the flowers became symbolical of a great release, of a wonderful awakening. My eyes had all at once been opened; till then I had walked in darkness, yet knew it not. (*Ryecroft* 22-23)

This almost religious rapture is shared by all of Orwell's protagonists. John Flory escapes the bitter racism of the European Club for the enchanted beauty of the Burmese jungle where he is inspired by exotic plants and wildlife. Accompanied by his girl friend, cynical Gordon Comstock, like Ryecroft, is invigorated by a country ramble. Outside of London, Comstock "felt as though he had been living underground for a long time past. He felt etiolated and unkempt" (*Keep* 126). But once in the open fields, Gordon, like Henry Ryecroft, comes alive in the golden countryside, "The light came slanting and yellow across the fields, and delicate unexpected colours sprang out in everything, as though some giant's child had been let loose with a new paintbox" (*Keep* 127). Although December, it "was astonishingly warm, as warm as summer." Freed of London streets and dim rooms, Gordon and Rosemary enjoy a "sexless rapture" which leads the hack writer to announce, "'We'll burn a sacrifice to the immortal gods, presently'" (*Keep* 127).

This sense of religious awe is shared by Dorothy Hare who at one point before her amnesia attack draws a fennel against her face:

> Its richness overwhelmed her, almost dizzied her for a moment. She drank it in, filling her lungs with it. Lovely, lovely scent—scent of summer days, scent of childhood joys, scent of spice-drenched islands in the warm foam of oriental seas!
> Her heart swelled with sudden joy. It was that mystical joy in the beauty of the earth and the very nature of things that she recognised, perhaps mistakenly, as the love of God. . . . All the riches of summer, the warmth of the earth, the song of birds, the fume of cows, the droning of countless bees, mingling and ascending like the smoke of ever-burning altars. . . . She began to pray, and for a moment she prayed ardently, blissfully, forgetting herself in the joy of worship.

> Then, less than a minute later, she discovered that she was kissing the frond the fennel that was still against her face. (*Clergyman's* 64-65)

Even Orwell's pragmatic salesman, George Bowling, who cheerfully announces in *Coming Up for Air*, "I'm vulgar, I'm insensitive, and I fit in with my environment," is given to nature worship. Middle-aged, overweight, struggling to support a wife and two children on the brink of world war, he stops his car and picks primroses:

> I stayed there for a bit, leaning over the gate. I was alone, quite alone. I was looking at the field, and the field was looking at me. I felt—I wonder whether you'll understand. What I felt was something that's so unusual nowadays that to say it sounds like foolishness. I felt *happy*. . . . Seasonal effect on the sex-glands, or something. But there was more to it than that. . . .
> . . . . I only want to be alive. And I was alive that moment when I stood looking the primroses. . . It's a feeling inside you, a kind of peaceful feeling, and yet it's like a flame. (*Coming* 192-193)

His reverie broken by the approach of car, Bowling feels embarrassed about being seen as a fat man in a bowler hat picking primroses. Sensing that any other activity would rescue his dignity, he pretends to be doing up his fly as the car passes. For Bowling, living in the tense year of 1938, nature worship is something sentimental, something "sappy."

Orwell presents the most striking conflict between society and nature in *Nineteen Eighty-Four*. Living amid posters of Big Brother, blaring propaganda, the ubiquitous telescreens, Winston Smith takes refuges in dreams of nature:

> Suddenly he was standing on short springy turf, on a summer evening when the slanting rays of the sun gilded the ground. The landscape that he was looking at recurred so often in his dreams that he was never fully certain whether or not he had seen it in the real world. In his waking thoughts he called it the Golden Country. (29)

Meeting Julia in the countryside later in the novel, Smith actually discovers a pasture like the one in his dreams and declares it to be the Golden Country. Here, away from Big Brother's telescreens, Winston and Julia are free to be sexually active and be fully human.

For both Gissing and Orwell, nature plays an intrinsic role in human happiness, especially in romantic and sexual relationships. In *The Odd Women* Everard Barfoot and Rhoda Nunn express their love for each other while hiking through "'grand, wild country.'" The relationship between Nancy Lord and Lionel Tarrant flourishes during country walks. Nancy, in particular, relishes the blissful solitude nature offers:

> Here, in many a nook carpeted with softest turf, canopied with tangle of leaf and bloom, solitude is safe from all intrusion—unless it be that of a flitting bird, or of some timid wild thing that rustles for a moment and is gone. From dawn till midnight, as from midnight till dawn, one who would be alone with nature might count upon the security of these bosks and dells. (*Jubilee* 99)

Tarrant, who worships the sun like Henry Ryecroft, tells Nancy that sunshine is "indispensable to his life; he never passed the winter in London; if he were the poorest of mortals, he would, at all events, beg his bread in a sunny clime" (117). Celebrating nature, Tarrant at one point makes Nancy a crown of ivy. In *New Grub Street* natural beauty forms the setting of Harold Biffen's lonely suicide. Panged with unrequited love for Amy Reardon, Biffen decides to kill himself before the "warm, golden sunlight would disappear" (528). With "cherry countenance and eyes that gave sign of pleasure as often as they turned to the sun-smitten clouds" Biffen heads to the park, pausing to watch the river "with a quiet smile, and enjoying the splendour of the sky." As he reaches his destination, it grows dark and he is gripped by the beauty of the "new-risen moon, a perfect globe, vast and red." Moving to a secluded copse, he lies in the grass, contemplating the "placid sky." Taking poison, his last vision blends love and natural beauty, so that he sees Amy as a "star which had just come into his vision above the edge of dark foliage—beautiful, but infinitely remote" (529).

Orwell uses the couple in nature motif in three novels. In *Burmese Days* John Flory's relationship with Elizabeth intensifies on a hunting trip. Exploring the exotic Asian jungle together, they grow closer. Elizabeth feels "an extraordinary desire to fling her arms round Flory's neck and kiss him" (142). Gone is the stilted awkwardness that troubled Flory in town. Alone with Elizabeth in the jungle he senses their bond growing stronger:

> A sudden stillness came on them both, a sense of something momentous that must happen. Flory reached across and took her other hand. It came yieldingly, willingly. For a moment they knelt with their hands clasped together. The sun blazed upon them and the warmth breathed out of their bodies; they seemed to be floating upon clouds of heat and joy. He took her by the upper arms to draw her towards him.
> (144)

Similarly, Gordon Comstock and Rosemary have their happiest moments in *Keep the Aspidistra Flying* on a day trip to the country. Ironically, nature provides a more comforting environment to lovers on a December day than the city with its central heating and technological marvels:

> As the clouds melted away a widening yellow beam slid swiftly across the valley, gilding everything in its path. Grass that had been dull green shone suddenly emerald. The empty cottage below sprang out into warm colours, purply-blue of tiles, cherry-red of brick. Only the fact that no birds were singing reminded you that it was winter. Gordon put his arm round Rosemary and pulled her hard against him.
> (140)

For both Gissing and Orwell nature is not only important in what it represents in itself, a source of beauty, inspiration, and private contemplation, but what it stands in contrast to—the soul-crushing ugliness of urban civilization.

In all of Orwell's novels, as in most of Gissing's, London appears almost as a character—a dark, inhuman soot-stained heap of brick inhabited by deformed, often loathsome creatures. Orwell uses the word "etiolated" to describe both Gordon Comstock and Winston Smith who are weakened and dehumanized by the artificiality of modern urban life.

For both Gissing and Orwell, London was a place their characters wanted to escape. In *The Whirlpool*, Gissing's protagonist urges a friend to leave the city, "'Take a cottage and grow cabbages; dig for three hours a day. It would do you no end of good'"(91). Harvey Rolfe diagnoses his friend as suffering from an urban malady, "'Come along with me, and get the mephitis blown out of you. You've got town-disease, street-malaria, lodging house fever'" (91). Rolfe later suffers from another urban malady produced in the great loneliness of London:

> . . . his house was a shelter, a camp; granted a water-tight roof, and drains not immediately poisonous, what need to take thought for artificial comforts? Thousands of men, who sleep on the circumference of London, and go each day to business, are practically strangers to the district nominally their home; ever ready to strike tent, as convenience bids, they can feel no interest in a vicinage which merely happens to house them for the time being, and as often as not they remain ignorant of the names of streets or roads through which they pass in going to the railway station. Harvey was now very much in this case. . . .
>
> By force of habit he continued to read, but only books from the circulating library, thrown upon his table pell-mell—novels, popular science, travels, biographies; each as it came to hand. The intellectual disease of the time took hold upon him: he lost the power of mental concentration, yielded to the indolent pleasure of desultory page-skimming. (381)

Commenting to a friend on the landscape, he asserts that "a bit of ploughed field in the midlands" offers him more pleasure than the land which had once been beautiful "before London breathed upon it" (388). As in his other books, Gissing celebrates any contact with nature. Basil Morton enjoys his job as a grain merchant because his work brings him in touch with nature:

> "I like my trade," he said once to Harvey Rolfe; "it's clean and sweet and useful. The Socialist would revile me as a middleman; but society can't do without me just yet, and I ask no more than I fairly earn. I like turning over a sample of grain; I like the touch of it, and the smell of it. It brings me near to the good old Mother Earth, and makes me feel human." (323)

In a like manner, Orwell celebrates Dorothy Hare's exhausting migrant work as a hop picker. This back-breaking labor offers her more peace, more joy than urban life:

> It was stupid work, mechanical, exhausting and every day more painful to the hands, and yet you never wearied of it; when the weather was fine and the hops were good you had the feeling that you could go on picking for ever and for ever. It gave you a physical joy, a warm satisfied feeling inside you, to stand there hour after hour, tearing off the heavy clusters and watching the pale green pile grow higher and higher in your bin, every bushel another twopence in your pocket.
> (Clergyman's 127)

Orwell's Depression-era novels—*Keep the Aspidistra Flying* and *A Clergyman's Daughter*—and *Nineteen Eighty-Four* echo Gissing's in their depictions of London's grimy slums, friendless streets, foul taverns, odious drunks, dim shops, and depressing fog. The London Orwell envisioned in the future was a "grimy landscape" marked by "vistas of rotting nineteenth-century houses, their sides shored up with balks of timber, their windows patched with cardboard and their roofs with corrugated iron. . ." (7). It differs little from the London Gissing describes in *The Nether World* with its "millions of tons of brute brick and mortar, crushing the spirit as you gaze" (274).

In addition to a shared vision of the oppressive nature of the soul-crushing poverty of the slums, Gissing and Orwell voiced a common distaste for the ugly pretensions of the lower middle class. Both decried middle-class developments as the ugly embodiment of a tasteless class. Besides denouncing the soulless slums, *The Nether World* provides a grim view of the ever-expanding London suburbs:

> Look at a map of greater London, a map on which the town proper shows as a dark, irregularly rounded patch against the whiteness of suburban districts, and just on the northern limit of the vast network of streets you will distinguish the name of Crouch End. Another decade, and the dark patch will have spread greatly further; for the present, Crouch End is still able to remind one that it was in the country a very short time ago. The streets have a smell of newness, of dampness; the bricks retain their complexion, the stucco has not rotted more than one expects in a year or two; poverty tries to hide itself with venetian blinds, until the time when an advanced guard of houses shall justify the existence of the slum.
>   Characteristic of the locality is a certain row of one-story cottages—villas, the advertiser calls them—built of white bricks, each with one bay window on the ground floor, a window pretentiously fashioned as desiring to be taken for stone, though obviously made of bad plaster. Before each house is a garden measuring six feet by three, entered by a little iron gate, which grinds as you push it, and at no time would latch. The front-door also grinds on the sill; it can only be opened by force, and quivers in a way that shows how unsubstantially it is made.
>   As you set foot in the pinched passage, the sound of your tread proves the whole fabric a thing of lath and sand. The ceilings, the walls, confess themselves neither water-tight nor air-tight.
>   Whatever you touch is at once found to be sham. (364)

For Gissing the enemy is not only the slums housing exploited workers, but the city itself, its streets and houses spreading like a cancer into the countryside. George Bowling, Orwell's obese salesman, shares this view, seeing his London suburb as a "festering" force:

> You know how these streets fester all over the inner-outer suburbs. Always the same. Long, long rows of little semi-detached houses . . . as much alike as council houses and generally uglier. The stucco front, the creosoted gate, the privet hedge, the green front door. . . . A line of semi-detached torture chambers where the poor little five-to-ten-pound-a-weekers quake and shiver. . .
> Every one of those poor downtrodden bastards, sweating his guts out to pay twice the proper price for a brick doll's house that's called Belle Vue because there's no view and the bell doesn't ring—every one of those poor suckers would die on the field of battle to save his country from Bolshevism. (*Coming* 11-15)

In *Coming Up for Air*, Orwell sought to satirize middle class Britain on the brink of the Second World War. Many of its passages mirror Gissing's novel *In the Year of the Jubilee*. Both novels dwell on sham architecture, bad literature, advertising, and the destruction of nature by middle class housing developments.

Gissing describes Jessica living in a home favoring "neither health nor mental tranquillity." It is not a slum, but a new suburban house, the dream home of an expanding middle class:

> It was one of a row of new houses in a new quarter. A year or two ago the site had been an enclosed meadow, a portion of the land attached to what was once a country mansion; London, devourer of rural limits, of a sudden made hideous encroachment upon the old estate, now held by a speculative builder; of many streets to be constructed, three or four had already come into being, and others were mapped out, in mud and inchoate masonry, athwart the ravaged field. Great elms, the pride of generations passed away, fell before the speculative axe, or were left standing in mournful isolation to please a speculative architect; bits of wayside hedge still shivered in fog and wind, amid hoardings variegated with placards and scaffolding black against the sky. The very earth had lost its wholesome odour; trampled into mire, fouled with builders' refuse and the noisome drift from adjacent streets, it sent forth, under the sooty rain, a smell of corruption, of all the town's un-cleanliness. On this rising locality had been bestowed the title of "Park." (*Jubilee* 196-197)

And once housed in the Park, the inhabitants discover their new homes to be nightmare constructions which begin to crumble in the first winter.

Returning to Lower Binfield after an absence of thirty years, George Bowling discovers that his quaint farm town has mushroomed into a mid-sized commercial center. Atop a hill dotted with "fake-picturesque houses," Bowling looks down, unable to find familiar landmarks, "All I could see was an enormous river of brand-new houses" and "two enormous factories of glass and concrete" (*Coming* 211).

Like Gissing, Orwell's protagonist views urbanization as a malevolent force. "Houses, shops, cinemas, chapels, football grounds—new, all new," Bowling notes. "Again I had that feeling of a kind of enemy invasion having happened behind my back. All these people flooding in from Lancashire and the London suburbs, planting themselves down in this beastly chaos, not even bothering to know the chief landmarks of the town by name" (215). Like the London suburbs described in *In the Year of the Jubilee*, Lower Binfield has bloomed with newness and shoddiness:

> And the newness of everything! The raw, mean look! Do you know the look of these new towns that have suddenly swelled up like balloons in the last few years, Hayes, Slugh, Dagenham and so forth? The kind of chilliness, the bright red brick everywhere, the temporary-looking shop-windows full of cut-price chocolates and radio parts. (215)

Returning to the Thames where he fished as a boy, Bowling finds the once remote riverbank "black with people." Water-meadows have been replaced by a clutter of "tea-houses, penny-in-the-slot machines, sweet kiosks and chaps selling Wall's Ice Cream" (238). Instead of isolated fishermen, "there was a continuous chain of men fishing, one every five yards" (238-239). The river, which once was luminous green with darting fish is now "brown and dirty, with a film of oil on it from the motorboats, not to mention the fag-ends and the paper bags" (239).

Searching for the secluded pool where he caught his first fish as a boy, Bowling enters a pretentious housing development not unlike "the Park" Gissing described a half-century before. "It was all houses, houses, houses," Bowling laments (252). As in Gissing's nineteenth century development, "All the woods that used to grow beyond the pool, and grew so thick that were like a kind of tropical jungle, had been shaved flat. Only a few clumps of trees still standing round the houses. There were arty-looking houses, another of those sham-Tudor colonies. . ." (252-253). Bowling views the prim estate with despair:

> There was nothing left of the woods. It was all houses, houses—and what houses! Do you know these faked-up Tudor houses with the curly roofs and the buttresses that don't buttress anything, and the rock-gardens with concrete bird-baths and those red plaster elves you can buy at the florists'? You could see in your mind's eye the awful gang of food-cranks and spook-hunters and simple-lifers with 1,000 pounds a year that lived there. Even the pavements were crazy. . . . Some of the houses made me wish I'd got a hand-grenade in my pocket. (255)

Discovering his favorite pool drained to serve as a trash pit for sham-Tudor houses, Bowling cries out against progress and development, savoring trees over people just as Eldon prefers grass over the workers in *Demos*:

> And they'd filled my pool up with tin cans. God rot them and bust them! Say what you like—call it silly, childish, anything—but doesn't it make you puke sometimes to see what they're doing to England, with their bird-baths and their plaster gnomes, and their pixies and tin cans, where the beechwoods used to be?
> Sentimental, you say? Anti-social? Oughtn't to prefer trees to men? I say it depends what trees and what men. Not that there's anything one can do about it, except to wish them the pox in their guts. (257)

For both Gissing and Orwell, the future holds promise of a world deprived of beauty in the name of smoky factories and artificially lighted pleasure domes. Gissing's adman Luckworth Crewe outlines plans for a seaside exhibition pier:

> He unrolled a large design, a coloured picture of Whitsand pier as it already existed in his imagination. Not content with having the mere structure exhibited, Crewe had persuaded the draughtsman to add embellishments of a kind which, in days to come, would be his own peculiar care; from end to end, the pier glowed with the placards of advertisers. Below, on the sands, appeared bathing-machines, and these also were covered with manifold advertisements. Nay, the very pleasure-boats on the sunny waves declared the glory of somebody's soap, of somebody's purgative.
> "I'll make that place one of the biggest advertising stations in England—see if I don't! You remember the caves? I'm going to have them lighted with electricity, and painted all round with advertisements... " (386).

There is little difference between Luckworth Crewe's electric cave and the pleasure spots Orwell noted as postwar dream developments. In the hands of entrepreneurs, Orwell noted the natural pleasure dome of Kubla Khan would be rendered into Luckworth's cave—"caverns, air-conditioned, discreetly lighted and with their original rocky interior buried under layers of tastefully-coloured plastics, would be turned into a series of tea-grottoes in the Moorish, Caucasian or Hawaiian styles" (*CEJL* IV 79). In these artificial worlds, the regulated light and temperature rob people of contact with the natural world. Piped in music serves to cancel out conversation and in Orwell's words, "prevents the onset of that dreaded thing, thought" (*CEJL* IV 80).

The theme of nature is central to both Gissing's and Orwell's thought and politics, illustrating their sense that their worlds were traveling into inhospitable regions. Modern life was increasingly ugly, inhumane, and thought deadening. The future, though better lighted and more comfortable, promised to be an alienating and oppressive environment for people who wanted to retain their individuality. Progress, invention, development—whether run by admen and entrepreneurs or Utopian dreamers and Socialists—promise to rob humanity of its contact with nature. For Orwell and Gissing, both agnostics, nature was a source of spiritual strength, honesty, and integrity offering a respite from a dehumanizing civilization.

NINE
CONCLUSION

> ... part of the charm of Gissing is that he belongs so unmistakably to his own time, although his time treated him badly.
>
> George Orwell

For over half a century, critics have attempted to explain Orwell's contradictory character by analogy. The "real Orwell" is not a Socialist, it is declared, but an existentialist like Camus or a believer in the underdog version of morality along the lines of Dickens or Simone Weil. Such comparisons, however, can distort as well as illuminate. Other figures are themselves given to complexity and cannot always serve as fixed points to chart an unknown.

The striking parallels between Gissing and Orwell reveal much about Orwell's thought and character. But Orwell was *not* Gissing. Gissing abandoned his youthful flirtation with political ideology to cultivate the sensibilities of the intellectually superior individual who shuns public life and party affiliations. Orwell remained a dedicated, if often disillusioned, Socialist. In his essays and non-fiction books, Orwell outlined his beliefs in a humanistic form of Socialism based on common decency and universal brotherhood rather than Marxist doctrine:

> There is [little] question now of averting a collectivist society. The only question is whether it is to be founded on willing co-operation or on the machine-gun. The Kingdom of Heaven, old style, has definitely failed, but on the other hand "Marxist realism" has also failed, whatever it may achieve materially. (*CEJL* II 16-17)

For Orwell the solution was a faith in humanity, a sense of universal brotherhood. "People sacrifice themselves for the sake of fragmentary communities—nation, race, creed, class—and only become aware that they are not individuals in the very moment when they are facing bullets," Orwell observed. "A very slight increase of consciousness, and their sense of loyalty could be transferred to humanity itself," he argued (*CEJL* II 17). Gissing, Orwell observed, did not share these concerns:

> Gissing would have liked a little more money for himself and some others, but he was not much interested in what we should now call social justice. He did not admire the working class as such, and he did not believe in democracy. He wanted to speak not for the multitude, but for the exceptional man, the sensitive man, isolated among barbarians.(*CEJL* IV 430)

Orwell was also slightly dismissive of what he presumed to be Gissing's desired existence. "His ideal, a rather melancholy one," Orwell noted, "was to have a moderate private income and live in a small comfortable house in the country, preferably unmarried, where he could wallow in books, especially the Greek and Latin classics" (*CEJL* IV 435).

What Orwell did admire about Gissing was his power as a novelist of the individual. All of Orwell's novels concern the plight of individuals in hostile environments, ranging from the racist small-minded world of colonial Burma to the frigid brutalities of Oceania in 1984. In his fiction, Orwell's faith in Socialism with a human face is totally absent. In novels, Orwell spoke for the individual not humanity. The Depression-era novels are uncharacteristic for a Socialist. Gordon Comstock quits his job to wage a smug money-strike totally unaware of the hundreds of thousands of unemployed suffering around him. When his girl friend becomes pregnant, he goes back to his old job, enjoying the indulgent unconditional love of an employer who holds a position open for a marginal employee in the depths of a worldwide Depression. Dorothy Hare's spiritual battle takes place in a void, totally apart from the theological and ideological forces raging about her. The novel could have just as easily been set in the nineteenth century. For a writer whose essays tracked current events, Orwell did not seek to make standard political arguments. George Bowling, for instance, is not caught up in the doctrinal battle of Left and Right on the brink of World War II but ponders the coming "after war" and bitterly comments on processed food and the loss of a boyhood fishing hole. There is no attempt to fictionalize a social ill or dramatize a political point by creating a microcosm. Orwell never presents characters who represent a class or group, but individuals, eccentric and sometimes irritating characters, who like Gissing's, try to make their way in inhospitable worlds. For Orwell, the novel had a special definition:

> The word "novel" is commonly used to cover almost any kind of story—*The Golden Asse, Anna Karenina, Don Quixote, The Improvisatore, Madame Bovary, King Solomon's Mines* or anything else you like—but it also has a narrower sense in which it means something hardly existing before the nineteenth century and flourishing chiefly in Russia and France. A novel, in this sense, is a story which attempts to describe credible human beings, and—without necessarily using the technique of naturalism—to show them acting on everyday motives and not merely undergoing strings of improbable adventures. . . . If one accepts this definition, it becomes apparent that the novel is not an art-form in which England has excelled. (*CEJL* IV 433)

But for Orwell there was one English writer who did excel at writing novels, George Gissing:

> The writers commonly paraded as "great English novelists" have a way of turning out either not to be true novelists, or not to be Englishmen. Gissing was not a writer of picaresque tales, or burlesques, or comedies, or political tracts: he was interested in individual human beings, and the fact that he can deal sympathetically with different sets of motives, and makes a credible story out of the collision between them, makes him exceptional among English writers. (*CEJL* IV 434)

In estimating Gissing's importance, Orwell concluded, "we must be thankful for the piece of youthful folly" that derailed his academic career and "forced him to become the chronicler of vulgarity, squalor and failure" (*CEJL* IV 436).

For Orwell, Gissing was a model of the kind of novelist he wanted to be, a writer who explored the status of individual identity in the twentieth century. Like Gissing, he was a "chronicler of vulgarity, squalor and failure" and like Gissing, Orwell "belongs . . . to his own time, although his time treated him badly" (*CEJL* IV 434).

To understand Orwell fully, one must first read Gissing.

BIBLIOGRAPHY

Alldritt, Keith. *The Making of George Orwell*. London: Edward Arnold, 1969.

Ashe, Geoffrey. "A Note on George Orwell." *Commonweal* 54 1951: 191-193.

Beadle, Gordon. "George Orwell and the Death of God." *Colorado Quarterly* 23 1974: 51-63.

Bergonzi, Bernard. Introduction. *New Grub Street*. By George Gissing. New York: Penguin, 1985. 9-26.

Carter, Michael. *George Orwell and the Problem of Authentic Existence*. Totowa, New Jersey: Barnes and Noble, 1985.

Connelly, Mark. *The Diminished Self: Orwell and the Loss of Freedom*. Pittsburgh: Duquense University Press, 1987.

Coppard, Audrey and Bernard Crick, ed. *Orwell Remembered*. New York: Facts on File, 1984.

Coustillas, Pierre and Colin Partridge, ed. *Gissing: The Critical Heritage*. London: Routledge & Kegan Paul, 1985.

Crick, Bernard. *George Orwell: A Life*. Boston: Little and Brown, 1980.

Dickens, Charles. *Oliver Twist*. New York: Harper and Row, 1965.

Donnelly, Mabel. *George Gissing: Grave Comedian*. Cambridge: Harvard University Press, 1954.

Fink, Howard. "*Coming Up for Air:* Orwell's Ambiguous Satire on the Wellsian Utopia." *Studies in Literary Imagination*. vol

vi. no. 2 1973: 51-60.

Gissing, George. *Born in Exile*. London: Howgarth Press, 1985.

———*Charles Dickens: A Critical Study*. London: Gresham Publishing Company, 1903.

———*The Collected Letters of George Gissing*. ed by Paul F Mattheisen, Arthur C. Young, and Pierre Coustillas. vol 1-6. Athens, Ohio: Ohio University Press, 1990.

———*Demos*. London: Smith, Elder, and Co., 1897.

———*George Gissing and H. G. Wells: Their Friendship and Correspondence* ed. Royal A. Gettman. Urbana: University of Illinois Press, 1961.

———*George Gissing's Commonplace Book: A Manuscript in the Berg Collection of the New York Public Library*. ed. Jacob Korg. New York: New York Public Library, 1962.

———*In the Year of the Jubilee*. New York: Dover, 1982.

———*Letters of George Gissing to Eduard Bertz 1887-1903*. ed. Arthur Young. New Brunswick: Rutgers University Press, 1961.

———*Letters of George Gissing to Members of his Family*. Collected and arranged by Algernon and Ellen Gissing. London: Constable, 1972.

———*A Life's Morning*. Brighton: Harvester Press, 1984.

———*London and the Life of Literature in the Late Victorian England: The Diary of George Gissing, Novelist*. ed. Pierre Coustillas. Hassocks: Harvester Press, 1978.

———*The Nether World*. London: Dent, 1973.

———*New Grub Street*. New York: Penguin, 1985.

———*The Odd Women*. New York: W. W. Norton, 1971.

———*The Private Papers of Henry Ryecroft*. Oxford: Oxford University Press, 1987.

———*The Whirpool*. London: Hogarth Press, 1984.

———*Workers in the Dawn*. Brighton: Harvester Press, 1985.

Goode, John. *George Gissing: Ideology and Fiction*. New York: Barnes and Noble, 1978.

Grylls, David. *The Paradox of Gissing*. London: Allen and Unwin, 1968.

Guild, Nicholas. "In Dubious Battle: George Orwell and the Victory of the Money-God." *Modern Fiction Studies*. Spring, 1975: 49-56.

Halperin, John. *Gissing: A Life in Books*. Oxford: Oxford University Press, 1987.

Hammond, J. R. *A George Orwell Companion*. London: Macmillian, 1982.

Jain, Jasbir. "Orwell: The Myth of a Classless Society." *Quest*. 72 1971: 95-100.

Kirk, Russell. "George Orwell's Despair." *Intercollegiate Review*. 1968: 21-25.

Korg, Jacob. *George Gissing: A Critical Study*. Seattle: University of Washington Press, 1963.

Kubal, David L. *Outside the Whale: George Orwell's Art and Politics*. Notre Dame: University of Notre Dame Press, 1972.

Meyers, Jeffrey, ed. *Orwell: The Critical Heritage* London: Routledge and Kegan Paul, 1975.

----*A Reader's Guide to George Orwell*. London: Thames and Hudson, 1975.

Orwell, George. *Animal Farm*. New York: New American Library, 1946.

----*Burmese Days*. New York: New American Library, 1963.

----*A Clergyman's Daughter*. New York: Harcourt Brace, 1960.

----*The Collected Essays, Journalism and Letters of George Orwell*. ed. Sonia Orwell and Ian Angus. vol 1-4 New York: Harcourt Brace, 1968. (*CEJL*)

----*Coming Up For Air*. New York: Hacourt Brace.

----*Down and Out in Paris and London*. New York: Harcourt Brace.

----*Keep the Aspidistra Flying*. New York: Harcourt Brace, 1956.

———*Nineteen Eighty-Four*. New York: New American Library, 1961.

———*The Road to Wigan Pier*. New York: Berkeley, 1967.

Powell, Anthony. "George Orwell A Memoir." *Atlantic Monthly*. CCXX October 1967: 62-68.

Pritchett, V. S. "1984." *Twentieth Century*. 20-24.

Rees, Richard. *George Orwell: Fugitive From the Camp of Victory*. Carbondale: Southern Illinois University Press, 1962.

Rodden, John. *The Politics of Literary Reputation: The Making and Claiming of "St. George" Orwell*. New York: Oxford University Press, 1989.

Sandison, Alan. *The Last Man in Europe*. London: Macmillian, 1974.

Selig, Robert. *George Gissing*. Boston: Twayne, 1983.

Sheldon, Michael. *Orwell: The Authorized Biography*. New York: HarperCollins, 1991.

Small, Christopher. *The Road to Miniluv*. Pittsburgh: University of Pittsburgh Press, 1975.

Stansky, Peter and William Abrahams. *Orwell: The Transformation*. New York: Knopf, 1980.

Swinnerton, Frank. *George Gissing: A Critical Study*. New York: Doran, 1927.

Tindall, Gillian. *The Born Exile: George Gissing*. London: Temple Smith, 1974.

Woodcock, George. *The Crystal Spirit: A Study of George Orwell*. New York: Schocken Books, 1984.

INDEX

Advertising, 7, 13, 20, 84, 108, 109, 112
Animal Farm, 1, 24, 83, 88, 89
Ashe, Gregory, 4
Auden-Isherwood, 7

Beadle, Gordon, 4
Bergonzi, Bernard, 11
Black, John George, 15
Born in Exile, 10, 22, 65
Burmese Days, 55-56, 58, 59, 60, 61, 81, 105

Carter, Michael, 5
Charles Dickens: A Critical Study, 31, 32
Childhood History of England, 33
Clergyman's Daughter, A, 11, 30, 63, 70, 82, 102-103, 107
Coming Up for Air, 12, 65, 103, 109, 110-117
Commercialism, 7, 20, 84, 108, 109, 110, 111
Communism, 1, 2

Demos, 24, 76, 78, 85-95, 97
Dickens, Charles, 25, 27-39
Oliver Twist, 29
Down and Out in Paris and London, 17

Frigidity, 71

Gandhi, Mahatma, 4
Gissing, Algernon, 20-21
Gissing, George
    America, travels to, 16-17

arrest for theft, 14-16
biography, 14-20
Born in Exile, 10, 22, 65
Charles Dickens: A Critical Study, 31, 32
democracy, view of, 24
Demos, 24, 76, 78, 85-95, 97
In the Year of the Jubilee, 66, 84, 104, 109-110
nature, view of, 97
Nether World, The, 29, 85, 104, 107, 108
New Grub Street, 10-11, 12, 24, 39, 40, 41, 42-45, 46-47
Odd Women, The, 10, 12, 24, 69-70, 75-82, 104
poor, attitudes toward, 20-21
poverty, 14-16, 24
Private Papers of Henry Ryecroft, The, 12, 98, 99, 100, 102
Whirlpool, The, 106
Workers in the Dawn, 17, 18, 29, 55, 57, 58, 59, 60
Good Rich Man, 34, 35

Halperin, Hohn, 13, 15, 16, 20, 21
"Hanging, A," 1

Harrison, Frederic, 18
Harrison, "Nell," 15-17, 18
Hitler, Adolf, 3-4

In the Year of the Jubilee, 66, 84, 104, 109-110
Industrialism, 3, 88, 94, 95

Jain, Jasbir, 4

Keep the Aspidistra Flying, 12, 22, 30, 39, 41, 43, 47-50, 63, 65, 102, 107
Kirk, Russell, 6
Korg, Jacob, 14, 17-18

Left Book Club, 2, 29-30
Lenin, 3
Life's Morning, A, 23
London slums, 29-31

Madonna-whore dichotomy, 57-59, 60
Marriage, 65-67, 71, 76-80
McHugh, Vincent, 11
Middle class tastes, 13, 108, 109, 111
Miller, Henry, 7
Muggeridge, Malcolm, 6

Nationalism, 4
Nature
  Gissing's views, 97
  Orwell's views, 100-107
Nether World, The, 29, 107, 108
New Grub Street, 10-11, 12, 24, 39, 40, 41, 42-45, 46, 47, 85, 104
Nineteen Eighty-Four, 11, 29, 30, 50, 54, 64, 103-104, 107
Nuremberg trials, 4

Odd Women, The, 10, 12, 24, 69-70, 75-82, 104
Oliver Twist, 29, 30
Orwell, George
  Animal Farm, 1, 24, 83, 88, 89
  biography, 9-10
  Burmese Days, 55-56, 58, 59, 60, 61, 81, 105
  Clergyman's Daughter, A, 11, 30, 63, 70, 82, 102-103
  Coming Up For Air, 12, 65, 103, 109, 110-117
  Dickens, views of, 33, 34, 35-37
  Dickens and Gissing, 25, 27
  Down and Out in Paris and London, 17
  existentialism, 5
  Gissing, views of, 9-12, 20, 25
  history, sense of, 2
  Keep the Aspidistra Flying, 12, 22, 30, 39, 41, 43, 47-50, 63, 65, 102, 107
  Nineteen Eighty-Four, 11, 29, 30, 50, 54, 64, 103-104, 107
  poverty, 13-14, 45-46
  Road to Wigan Pier, The, 2-3, 40, 75, 88, 99
  science and technology, 2 97-98
  sexuality, 54-55
  "Shooting an Elephant," 1
  Spanish Civil War, 9
Owens College, 15

Political correctness, 1, 3
Positivism, 17, 18, 85
Poverty, 13, 29, 30, 45-46, 48-49
Powell, Anthony, 1, 6
Pritchett, V. S., 9
Private Papers of Henry Ryecroft, The, 12, 98, 99, 100, 102
Prostitution, 15-18, 56

Rees, Richard, 5, 10, 12
"Revenge is Sour," 5
Roberts, Morley,
Road to Wigan Pier, The, 2-3, 40, 75, 88, 99

Science and technology, 2-3, 4
Selig, Robert, 11
Sex and money, 41-42, 64-65
Sexual frustration, 42, 46, 48-49, 53-54, 58
Sexuality, 54, 56-58
"Shooting an Elephant," 1
Socialism, 2-3, 85-86, 116
Stalinism, 1, 9
Stansky and Abrahams, 11, 41
Symons, Julian, 10

Tale of Two Cities, A, 32
Technology, 1, 3, 98

Underwood, Edith, 19

Whirlpool, The, 106
Wilde, Oscar, 7
Women, 53-55, 57-59, 69-70, 73

Workers in the Dawn, 17, 18, 29, 55, 57, 58, 59, 60
Writing, 39, 49-50, 100-101